A Peace of Me

A Black Man's Journey to Love and Commitment

Randall Courtland Davis

A Peace of Me, A Black Man's Journey to Love and Commitment
Copyright © 2021 Randall Courtland Davis

Published in the United States, Saintstown Productions.

Saints Town Productions
RandallCDavis.com

First Edition

ISBN: 978-1-7363706-1-2

Foreword

There comes a time for us all, when something causes us to press the pause button and take stock in where we are and how we see ourselves. This is called the journey of self-discovery. As a practicing marriage and family therapist for the last 16 years, I often work with clients as they embark upon this journey. Many of my clients find themselves at a crossroad as they begin to look back at past decisions that have led to their current situation. It is then that many of my clients want to bail, as they are not always ready to truly see themselves. Yet, this is when I tell them that the real work begins. That they will continue to find themselves in spaces and places that don't feed their Spirit, Soul, Mind and Body, if they do not complete this part of their journey of self-discovery.

We are constantly evolving as life, and experiences stagnate or mature us. This is an underlying theme of this piece of work that in each of the four sections: *In the Beginning, The Middle Passage, Seven Stories and With Maturity Comes...,* allows you to see the author demonstrate this as a father, partner, son and friend.

When on this journey of self-discovery, we find ourselves examining our relationships, both past and present, our choices, our decisions and the results that have brought us to the point of pressing the pause button. We start to consider if the relationships we are engaging in are fulfilling. We start to wonder if they are built solely upon chemistry and passion, which can fizzle over time. Or, are they built on compatibility, communication, and compassion, which creates long lasting connections? Then, this is when we start to ask ourselves if we want to continue to engage in situationships or work towards building connections of substance, both platonically and romantically. We start to wonder if the destination that we currently occupy is one of convenience, and if so, how long before it becomes too uncomfortable to stay put.

We start to be honest with ourselves and acknowledge that convenience is not love or loyalty. We start to ask ourselves how to right our wrongs if we are ready to engage in reconciliation conversations with those that we want to stay connected to or wish to be reconnected with.

This is where we begin the process of forgiveness and release ourselves from the shame and guilt that we carry in our emotional backpacks and choose not to be held hostage by our mistakes. We must then make the choice to stop jumping through hoops to make up for our past discretions and poor choices. And lastly, we discover that all conflict and confrontation is not bad; yet, resolution can come through uncomfortable conversations.

In "A Peace of Me," you're invited on the author's journey of self-discovery as he allows you to see him in the raw. Randall chronicles why and how his journey began, what he discovers about himself and how his journey of self-discovery can be of benefit to both Black women and men alike. This piece of work embodies the importance of the journey of self-discovery for Black women and men, and allows you to see what pressing the pause button and taking stock in where you are and how you see yourself, truly entails. Randall explores and connects to the journey of self-discovery, your faith, your spirit, unconditional love, being fully loved, following your dreams, gender restraints attributed to Black women and men being enslaved, soul care, words of wisdom and the seven aspects to creating a successful partnership.

As a Black woman who is also a therapist, wife, mother, daughter, and friend, I found this piece of work to be very loving, therapeutic, vulnerable, and considerate. And as you read these pages, you will discover that this piece of work is one of commitment and compassion which speaks to the hearts and minds of both Black women and men alike.

Blessings,

Wendy L. Whitmore, MS LMFT & Clinical Life Coach
CEO and Founder, WLW Healing House and
Truth Healing & Evolution Counseling Services

Contents

Dedicated to My Legacy

Ezra, Langston and Ramia

Acknowledgments

The Most High: Thank you for loving me and showing me favor and partnering together for your vision. Hallelujah to your name is the highest praise I can give you. You are forever and always sitting on the throne of my heart, guiding me to live according to your will.

Thank you Dad and Mom for your love, commitment and demonstration of what relationship and family can be. Your example and strength have been a source of strength and wisdom to me.

Thanks to my late sister, Rennell Davis-Franklin, for being my first best friend and a bright light to me, though she was born without sight.

I want to thank the handful of women, Queens, really, who shared themselves in relationship with me, and influenced my life in many ways. Although these relationships did not work out in the end, they were beautiful and taught me the meaning of reciprocity. In reflection, I can see what I did not do well, what I could have done better, and where I still have room for growth. It is in large part to you, and you know who you are that I remain grateful today.

As I am preparing to turn 56 at the completion of this book, I think about the women with whom I have had friendships over the past forty years. It is through them that I have learned further about spirituality, rejection, accountability, trust, vulnerability, acceptance, and how to become a more mature partner. Each of the incredible women allowed me to love them, and to be loved by them. I am profoundly grateful for them, and their bond; some of which have remained over our lifetime. I hope our endeavors together and apart assist each person reading on his/her journey…

I owe a considerable debt of gratitude to my writing coach. Jo Lena Johnson helped me clarify and flush out my thoughts and message. It was both therapeutic and amusing at times seeing the difference of what I wanted to say, and what I had written. I cannot thank her enough for her support, reassurance, and excitement for what I had to say. Thank you for the inspiration during each session.

Thanks to my friends, family and my "stand-in editors" Gwen Riles, Kennard Jones, and Tanayi Seabrook who had read portions of various drafts, and who were always encouraging and passionate about my journey.

My appreciation to Ramia Davis, Langston Davis, Danielle Hutchings, Shelbe Davis, Raymond and Aristean Davis, Kenya W. McKinney, Shawn Laususe, Geferol Mason, Falana Scott and Warren Cosey for being my supporters, and having my back. *Love you madly*.

Lastly, A huge thank you to Mrs. Jane Weisman, my 12th grade English teacher, who was the first person to believe in me as a writer. She told me I had something valuable to say, and that meant a lot.

Section One
In the Beginning

A person's foundation helps to determine how difficult or easy getting to destiny becomes; cultivation matters.

Greetings

In 2016, on a Sunday, I wrote a Facebook post starting with "Dear Future Wife," and what I would like to have said to her as a declaration of my love. I was not dating anyone, but I wanted to put it out there in case she was reading my post. I made a new post daily. By Wednesday, two childhood friends, who had not spoken to each other, texted me and asked the same question: "Are you writing a book?" The first text was from my play sister, Linda, "Cookie." Although I was confused by the text; the same was for Angie, my other play sister. After calling and talking with Angie, I took their inquiries as a sign that I was to write this book. I continued posting until that Saturday. With seven days of posting, I expounded on the posts and used them as chapters, and here we are.

I read a few self-help books after my divorce, and like many advent readers, I too was searching for support, clarity, and solutions to my personal story. I never imagined writing a book years later, but a revelation emerged. My promise to you? My experience, testimony, and truth will speak to something within you, aiding in the shift to the love you desire going forward. I believe you will get some insight, and nuggets of information, not just into my world, but also about Black men. This is an intimate peek into: struggles and misunderstandings, immaturity and growth, family and faith, marriage, divorce and parenting, societal influences, soul ties and the pursuit of success, partnership and friendship, seeking solace in identity and manhood, and the desire to seek out love again through my pursuit to heal and commit, beyond and despite the past. I am not a therapist, coach, or counselor. I am a Black man with some reflections that I choose to share because I revere *Black Love*!

Faith and Spirit

My faith is a personal relationship that reflects my walk with the Father and Son and Their importance of who they are to me. It is the reason I believe I was led to write this book. At times when I refer to The Most High, I will use the pronoun of Him/Her throughout the book, as Spirit that hovers over earth and is not simply masculine or feminine. I share this because if we continue to behave in the spirit of a patriarchal society, things will be uneven, conflict will continue, and understanding will wane. I am speaking about (God) which is a title, but refer to this entity in Hebrew as Yahawah, and His son, the Christ, as Yahawashi.

This book is my journey toward our understanding and relationship as partners with The Most High to become one soul, connected in Spirit. I believe because of the dominant patriarchal system, we men often have shown up chauvinists, emotionally unavailable, narcissistic, and controlling to our detriment. This is my attempt to say men are not here to hurt, but that we are of the same spirit; here to heal each other according to His/Her love for us.

Following My Dreams Changed Me

I have spent the past 29 years living in Los Angeles, with 12 of those working in Hollywood, writing scripts, and working on all-things creative. What I have learned is that when writing a story, many different characters must eventually be developed so that a complete and ably told story is presented. Well, that is the objective, but oftentimes that story and its characters falter, and you must do a rewrite. All noteworthy stories have multiple rewrites including yours and mine. As the hero of my love story, it is inevitable that I must look at my flaws for the story, to develop and improve. I believe my life is an Oscar-winning story, and not a straight-to-video or B-movie. So, my desire is to share the authentic, transparent experiences on my life's stage, so that perhaps you may see something to consider or mirror.

To tell my story, I have also shared poems from my adolescence. My poems were so authentically me that I wanted to include them in the book, so that you can see either my evolution or my return to the I am that I am; the essence of my authentic self. When I look back at them, I see me, the true me, before life and choices created multiple characters to fit multiple stories at the time. Why does this matter? Because like many, as I have matriculated through life, I have taken on different characteristics either trying to fit in, please, adapt, or protect myself from fears I had attached myself to.

Several chapters either start with a poem or end with prose I wrote over 40 years ago, coupled with lyrics of a song that made an indelible impression on my primary love language. At the time, *"Quality Time,"* followed by, *"Words of Affirmation,"* were my love languages that I discovered later in life from reading, *"The Five Love Languages,"* by Gary Chapman. It's funny how music can shape our idea of love; and, I was blessed to grow up in an era with great singers and lyrics that shaped how I would ultimately love the women who would be a part of my journey to find *my wife.*

I hope you are inspired to look at the pieces of your puzzle, seek wisdom and fit it all together in a way that is introspective, critical, and spiritual. It is through that intention that your story will also be Oscar-caliber.

Sankofa Love

Is an image of a bird walking in one direction with his head facing the opposite direction from whence it came with an egg in its mouth. The egg represents its history and origin. Its meaning represents our capture from Africa, and our enslavement in the Americas; thus, seeking our understanding and connection with our past to Africa. I wear this symbol as a necklace. It has a dual symbolic representation for me in seeking my wife and my reconnection with our homeland. I can't know whom I am to be with, nor do I know where I am in the process of seeing her until I revisit my past and make the connection to see and recapture the love for myself before loving someone else. This is my spiritual Sankofa love journey. To every man and woman seeking love today, I encourage you to reach back into your past, do the work of healing trauma, and restore that vision of partnership you desire for a better love tomorrow. We deserve it!

Fit the Description

My mission is Black men, and though this book is to Black women, I need Black men to be prepared to do what we have been called to do. We are to stand in it, to be available and to understand that we are the key to bringing the unity we had once upon a time. It is time to focus on the right things.

Brothers, when we selectively numb emotions such as vulnerability, fear, shame, anger etc., we also numb our joy, serenity, gratitude, and trust. Thus, choosing not to compromise is not having control; it is the opposite. It is time to be flexible. It is time for Black men to be who we truly are; no longer emulating what other cultures do, or who they are.

Black women have stood and helped keep us together. As our aborigine ancestors permitted, the woman would choose her mate. And, they would only choose the man who was the most responsible. In our history, African history, we traditionally had patriarchal societies, which had councils of women. The function of society, and the families were decided together inclusively, not exclusively.

I am not saying that women should rule the world. I am saying that we should come together and help each other. I believe that the Black man should protect the Black woman by all means necessary; and I believe that the Black woman should respect and honor the Black man in order to thrive.

Parental Guidance

When growing up, we tend to emulate, consciously or unconsciously what we see others do; and especially if it's positive, we tend to want it, too.

My parents are passionate with one another, romantic, connected and still making love at the age of 77, after 57 years of holy matrimony. I have fond memories of my parent's public displays of affection. I can remember being in the back seat of our car, not yet a teenager, watching my mom drop my dad off to work and the French kisses they would exchange like he was going off to war. Therefore, this public exchange of affection was natural to me. They were, and are, madly in love, and it shows! Recently, my mom told me that what kept their love ignited was that, "She drops it like it's hot!" Okay Ma! Then she got serious and shared the Three C's that have kept them in such a wonderful place: commitment, communication, and Christ. I am truly thankful for their love, example, and being great role models for marriage.

Keep It Simple Sweetheart (KISS)

Witnessing my parents' romance is probably why I love kissing more than anything!

In my experience, sex before you really know someone, even though it may be great, does not necessarily last. Getting to know the real person takes time; and exchanging kisses can teach us so much about one another. Therefore, I suggest remaining in the kissing stage as the bond grows. Sex can be an emotional crutch, especially if we become entangled in an early stage of the relationship. If you use sex as the go to for solving every fight or problem in life, it becomes an emotional thing you hold on to. If you do not have that, and simply kiss, it allows you to be more intimate and face what's happening in your life. Besides, sex is often seen differently by people, especially a man's perspective versus a woman's. Remember the old saying, "Why buy the cow when you can get the milk for free?" Remember that...

Be ready to kiss for long periods of time...

Seeds of Fatherhood

Ideas can be shaped early. However, real life can and should change our views as we mature.

Pre-sixteen, I had dreamed of having children, but I did not want to be married. At the time, I did not want to be responsible for a person, other than my children. I imagined having five kids and raising them by myself. I wanted a basketball squad, and five was the magic number.

I had been trying to get girls pregnant since I was sixteen. I once told a girlfriend that if she got pregnant, she should let me take care of the baby if she did not want to.

I wanted to be a different kind of father where I gave my kids freedom to be whoever and whatever he or she wanted. I understood that parents should provide a safe space for their children and not be reactive, resulting in the children mistrusting their parents with their thoughts. I knew I was not going to apply corporate punishment after 7 years of age. I wanted them to have opinions, ask tough questions and challenge authority; however, I never considered that they may question mine. Some questions may be uncomfortable, but it is your job to help modify what they think they know to what they should know. In my head, this was unorthodox in the Black community, but some "traditional" ideas just did not work for me. I never wanted to be that parent that said, "Do as I say, not as I do," or "Because I said so." Children are actors, and they act out what they see us do. I wanted to be a parent who asked my child, "son/daughter, what do you think about that?" Seven words that would help them to become more vulnerable, knowing that crying was okay; and feel safe to speak about thoughts/ideas that may be different. I wanted to be their friend as well as their "guidance counselor;" supporting them as they matriculated through life.

I also told myself that when I had my first kid, I was not going to work. The reason I did not want to work was because my dad worked a lot while I was growing up, and therefore, he didn't have a lot of time for me. I wanted more time with him; I loved him and just wanted more of him. I was a boy and wanted him to be at my basketball games and to hang out with me. He was busy teaching me tennis, chess, and yoga. That was okay, but I just wanted him to be at my games. Remember, I was a boy. So, to me, it seemed that when we were together, he reprimanded me and wanted to groom me instead of having fun, together. I did not want to repeat that pattern, so I told myself I would save the money I could so I would be "free" to be a present and fun dad. I started working at fifteen in preparation for my future and continued throughout high school, college and of course, after college.

As An Adult

Much later, during a therapy session, I was asked, "When was the first time you felt loved?" She told me not to harp on it, to simply give the first answer that came to mind.

My first thought? My dog Pebbles when I was six years old. I thought more about my answer, *And, why Pebbles, and not one of my parents?* It dawned on me that it was because I cared for her ever since she was a pup. I have always cared for people and animals, particularly those who could not care for themselves. At the time, I did not realize how much I did not like commitment. I did like the idea of romance and being the type of man that women desired; however, I was more of a Romeo, not a dog or player. I desired one woman at a time, except that one time. I have only cheated on a girl one time in my life, and that was in my early twenties. Lesson learned; never repeated.

I knew I was a little different than most of my male friends when it came to women. I was very carnal, at the same time, romantic. Based on what I learned from reading women's magazines, I assumed early on again that being responsible for another adult was not a job I wanted. It required a lot, but with kids I thought it only required me loving them and shaping them to be the best version of myself. Kahil Gibran, in *The Prophet* eloquently wrote that, "Our children do not belong to us." When I became a parent, I kept that in mind, wanting to give them what they needed to go out and do what they were destined to do.

The idea of having a partner, instead of just making babies changed a year later, when I fell for my first true love. Maybe because she was younger, I was able to love her in a more nurturing type of way; that was the beginning of wanting to be a nurturer and potential father.

Becoming a Father

When I had my first child, I was overjoyed. I stopped working to become a full-time father. My wife worked to support us for a short time. I can admit and truthfully say that raising a child 24/7 is a much more serious occupation than most people give it credit; it is a rigorous job.

Staying home with my daughter was the most fulfilling thing that had ever happened to me, and I would not have traded it for anything in the world. However, after a year of doing so, I could not wait to get back to work. When my next two kids were born, the experience was just as rewarding, though I did not choose to stay home with them. Reality set in, and I can admit that I enjoyed them more from the point of conception to about 12 years old, and then again after 21. Those teenage years were challenging! The reward was helping to mold them, not just with my words, but allowing my actions to be the examples which would ultimately safely shape them into the awesome young adults they are today. Being a father is an important job, and I have done my best.

Each child is different. You must meet them where they are emotionally and listen to their dreams while assessing them. It's important to help each recognize her/his gifts and purpose, fears and abilities; and to be like the Holy Spirit - guiding them, helping to navigate them to the top with fairness, and a firm hand.

In hindsight, I'm not sure what I was thinking when I wanted to raise kids by myself! Life showed me that it takes two, and children deserve to have both parents in the house. (And a village). Lovers should select wisely when deciding whom to go half on a baby with.

A Marriage Story

I had dreams of love and marriage without the context or proper foundation when I married my former wife. My three children, now young adults, are the beautiful fruit of our union, though she and I were not destined to spend our lives together.

Toward the end of my senior year at Clark-Atlanta, I left Georgia for an internship at Warner Brothers in the International Marketing Department located in Burbank, California. The year was 1990, and I had dreams of becoming an actor in Hollywood. I had hoped I could parlay my experience and budding opportunities into acting. However, I quickly realized that the level of performance and the expectation was quite different in Los Angeles, than it was in Atlanta. After the internship was over, instead of heading back to Georgia, I began working with a few production companies, including one owned by the legendary Quincy Jones. I met a young woman, who we will call Lilly, from the East Coast during that time. She had ambitions too, and her dreams were manifesting quicker than mine. I was smitten with her, so it made sense to work harder to support her dreams, as she was closer to manifesting her goals than I was at the time.

After the 7th day of working with her, I felt drawn to Lilly, and found her appealing in many ways. Yet, I was hesitant to get close to her, as I had been celibate, by choice, for a year. I wanted to be in a committed relationship and decided that spreading my seed would not allow me to be open to a true connection; the one meant for me. It felt like Lilly could be, "the one." I began praying to The Most High for guidance regarding her. Once her assignment was up, she returned to New York. We began courting, long distance, as she waited for her promised, permanent gig, that would bring her back to Los Angeles, and to me.

We got creative, accommodating the distance and the 3-hour time difference by ordering the same food, usually Chinese, renting the same movie from Blockbuster, and talking for hours. I could not wait to hold her in my arms, and was patiently waiting for her return.

Unbeknownst to me at the time, she headed to Las Vegas for the Tyson vs. Ruddock fight with her boss, with whom she had been in a relationship. I had no clue that she had been dating him, along with me. She used that trip as a catalyst to get closer to LA, to be with me. After the fight, she got a one-way ticket to Los Angeles, and she never left. Despite this revelation, I was all in. Lilly moved into my place. I supported her. The job she was counting on in L.A. fell through. That did not matter to me. Eight months later, we were married at City Hall in 1991. I was 27, and she was 22. *Were we in love?* Probably not, but at some point, we did fall in love for a time.

I realized I had lived my life on an idea of love, searching for acceptance. She was seeking love with no conditions, wanting to be seen, and validated. We found each other, like the lead characters in Quentin Tarantino's "True Romance."

Looking back, we probably had more good times than bad; the bad was bad and like most humans, we tend to see the bad worse than it really is, and never exalt the good. There were a few things that I could have done differently, but youth is a pitfall, and I didn't know any better.

I used to beat myself up. If I could tell my younger self one thing, it would be *forgive yourself.* We were living in Los Angeles, and I was working three jobs. She got a lucrative job which required her to move to Rome, Italy, for six months. We planned for the children and me to join her after she got settled and be there for five months with her, then for all of us to return to L.A. Just prior to her beginning that new job in Italy, my only sister died. Needless to say, it was a difficult time. Before the children and I met her in Rome, I made a decision without discussing it with her. I decided to pack up, put our things in storage, and after the six months were over, we would move to St. Louis to be closer to my parents, who were not handling my sister's death well. I felt they needed their only child and their grandchildren around them.

In hindsight, I believe this was the beginning of the end of our marriage because that decision crippled her career trajectory as St. Louis was not the place for her to thrive. I realize I put my need to be with my parents before our marriage and her career. In reflection, if I had it to do again, I would have been better at communicating. I would have figured out with her, how we could be close to my parents and how she could have returned to Los Angeles sooner, rather than later. There were a lot of options; however, I couldn't see them at the time, and regret how I allowed my heart and emotions to make such an important decision without her.

We returned to LA a year later. I found a good job; it was a good work space, I liked my immediate boss, and things were good for about a year. Then the company owner started doing some things which were racially biased, and not in my favor. Not one for biting my tongue, it became contentious, and I felt I had to quit, or it was going to end badly. My wife had been working a job that could support the family, so I quit without telling her. Figuring that I could stay home with the kids, we could get rid of the nanny and the gardener, and we would be better off.

Though she was making more money per week than most make in a month, she felt that a man should be a man and work; and that such a big decision should have been made together. She was correct, but again, I didn't see it that way. I was a young Black man and my anger and resentment at how I was being treated at my job showed me that I needed to be with my family, free, as opposed to putting hands on that guy, and risk not being locked up. I also felt that not working would allow me to do some things I had been wanting to do. Besides, who could raise my children better than me? Or, so I thought.

So, there I was home again caring for my children, I did not have to work, and I could start living out my dream of being a writer. Her public career was blossoming, and I was consumed with her success; taking an active role in helping her to advance. The only problem is that I lost myself in the process. I started being resentful and feeling like I could not get the breaks I wanted and deserved. I had supported the family for five years while she built her career. I wrote multiple scripts, had readings, and could not break into the private club. She began to look down on me, implying I wasn't man enough. I felt like I did not receive support, especially from her. And, when her job ended after 3 years, she was no longer interested in being married, saying that she was no longer in love. She said she fell out of love.

We had been married for nearly 10 years. I sought marriage counseling and asked her to join. I thought the sessions were for us to work on our marriage; however, she only wanted to be counseled on how to be better co-parents. Once I realized it was not about us, I decided to seek counseling on my own, knowing our relationship had run its course. We got divorced in August of 2001.

Counseling helped me, and of the many things I learned from speaking out loud, there were three major revelations:

1. I had an insatiable need to be a savior to women.
2. I had not grieved my sister's death.
3. I had put my children's mother on a pedestal. Doing so had diminished how I saw myself; in other words, I built her up to the detriment of my own worth.

The third issue was revealed to me in counseling with my pastor at the time. I'm sharing this because sometimes we need psychology, and sometimes we need Spiritual counseling.

After the Marriage

Though we were no longer together, those words and the way she looked at me continued to affect the way I saw myself for some time. Whenever a woman tells a man to "be a man," or "act like a man," it causes pain. I don't know if women realize they are weaponizing that phrase, and it is hurtful. Unfortunately, I allowed her assessment of me to define me. It would take years to shake off what had been planted, but I kept telling myself, my children, and anyone else who would listen, "Never let anyone define you."

During the marriage, I had gotten "comfortable and fat," without realizing it. I lost 25 pounds on the 'depression diet,' as I was going through the breakup. I was distraught. I was 37 years old and found myself homeless, couch surfing for seven months, and for one month, living in my car. In the divorce, all I wanted was joint custody of our children. At one point, she asked for the car I had. I gave it to her.

An interesting thing about being homeless, I was at my most peaceful, and I felt true contentment for the first time. I focused my time on reading the Word; the material things didn't affect me since I had nothing, and no distractions.

My children were so supportive even though I could only pick them up on weekends. The fact that I was a stay-at-home dad for the last year and half of our marriage. That relationship fully bonded me with my children and help me not go down the pity party road. I knew no one was bringing presents, so I had to push on. I let them know that I was living in my car. They were nine, seven and three years old. They thought it was "cool" living in the car. My daughter put her arms around me as I sat on the sand in the park and said, "You're a good dad!" I lost it and cried like a man, silently and privately. My children were my saving grace and sustained me through it all.

The key for me is I stayed active. I searched for a job, got government assistance, and shared what I had with my ex-wife. I remained busy with my church, working on the Mentorship Program, I helped curate, the Men's Choir, Sunday School, Dance Ministry, as well as studying for ministry.

I developed routines when I was living in my car. I had a family YMCA membership, and I would go to my storage unit, grab work out and interview clothes, workout, shower and then go to the kids' school. After a couple of hours volunteering in each of their classrooms, I would go to the resource center on Sunset Boulevard, use their computers, submit job applications and go on interviews...nothing. No job for eight months.

By this time, my long flowing locs were down to my waist. I eventually had to cut them. I had kept them because of vanity and needing to feel desired which was the only compensation I thought I needed, due to thinking I was not loved by the person I thought would love me forever.

The Most High told me to cut my locs, but I held on to them for another year. My disobedience had certainly contributed to the length of my peril. Once I became obedient, things changed. Through the grace of Yahawah, I was given two different cars during this time. I even got to the point that people were asking me to stay with them, which was a mutual blessing.

Once I cut my locs off, I got a great job and found a place to live; a home. It was fun getting the kids and going out to dinner, movies, and taking trips. My children's mother would call me "Disney Dad," yet, that was not meant to be endearing. When we divorced, we agreed to joint custody, and that is all I wanted. She kept the house and everything in it, except for a few paintings and several African artifacts. Co-parenting did not go well. I made the best of it, and in 2008, she violated the agreement by keeping our youngest child for seven months longer than was arranged out of school and in another country. I fought diligently to get him back, and I did March of 2009. I wanted and got full custody of our kids. They were nine, fourteen and fifteen.

What I Now Know

In the last two years of our marriage, financial difficulties seemed to lead to our dissolution. In hindsight, it was the lack of communication, commitment and being unequally yoked. Financial instability was an issue not only for a growing family, but also for the security and stability that women desire. When deciding on a partner, what I have learned is being equally yoked is essential. Meaning, you and your spouse share the same spiritual beliefs, have a level of commitment to each other's dreams, share similar family and parental values and know that societal roles do not dictate how you run your household.

It is about adapting, adjusting, and adhering to a communication that is respectful and honest. Lastly, when it comes to finances, all money is family money.

The Three C's

Communication

Communication should be an active, direct, honest, respectful, and transparent exchange of information, which is vital for a healthy relationship. When effectively communicating, one should also be mindful of tone. Men may 'hear nagging' when a woman may be 'speaking her feelings' or expressing her thoughts about something he may or may not have done because we receive and send words differently. Men also speak fewer words than women in general, which can be frustrating to women because they are accustomed to speaking more and hearing less. Our silence conveys messaging that should be spoken about as well; and in general, we really should do better as men. This all takes effort, practice, and time.

Therefore, do not take it personally, show kindness by asking questions, so that it is clear what is happening in the discourse. Own up to what you say, mean what you say, and be accountable with your words. We cannot be afraid to ask for clarity and she/he should not be offended when misunderstood.

Being an active listener is the highest praise you can pay a person. It will cut down some of the conflict when you repeat back what you heard. I know as men, we tend to say exactly what our woman had previously said, but in a different way. I am told that it is called "mansplaining." It is also passive listening. So, to avoid merely repeating what is said, listen closely and share how it makes you feel, respectfully. Repeating back what you heard, and interpreting what you believe the intended message was, gives you both the opportunity to clear up any gaps, miscommunication, or misinterpretation.

This type of communication from both partners shows validation of the other person's feelings and thoughts. You are acknowledging you hear them, and you should follow up with what you are planning to do about it, after getting clarity that you are both on the same page.

Heads up... I believe "the evil one" is constantly battling for our attention, and the goal is to steal, kill and destroy our joy; if we are aware of this, we can take steps to protect ourselves from injuries easily caused by conflict and miscommunication.

As we improve our communication and learn to be vulnerable to love, finding strength in what and how we share things with one another, we become like-minded and powerful together. It is important to communicate our love to each other with impeccable delivery. It will not be simple, but it must be deliberate. Let's make *this type of vulnerability* the new sexy.

One key thing about communication is the ability to reach resolve and to let go of attachments to 'being right.' We should not want to hold hostage the feeling of not being heard over the ones we love to feel good about ourselves. There are many books on how to let go of disagreements due to ego which often keeps us in conflict.

In the book, *The Mastery of Love,* by Don Miguel Ruiz; he writes about letting go of attachments. He believes you can begin each day a new day at a higher level of love because your reactions are the key to your happiness; therefore, you make that decision each day. I have learned a lot about the challenges we place on ourselves through ego, failed communication and not letting go, that results in unhealthy relationships.

Communication requires being vulnerable, uncomfortable, and sharing like-minded ideas/dreams that point us in the right direction, which is toward the top.

Christ

In terms of spiritual or religious faith, my partner will be a woman who seeks the Truth, is willing to do deeper research and come to an understanding for herself; not what someone has told her. I realize she may come from a Christian belief system, and that is okay, if she is open to exploring beyond the confines of the traditional patriarchal system or 'religiosity.' When I say the word Christ, I am saying this is the Messiah, and that He is the son of The Most High. I am a Believer, though I do not classify myself a Christian. I say that because I do not follow religious dogma, but instead read, research and seek the truth for myself for my personal relationship. Man's dogma tends toward classifying women as subordinates and serving individual desires for control and power, rather than following spiritual teaching and guidance for life. I do read the Hebrew Bible; the Tanakh, the Old Testament, and scripture primarily found in the Torah, the first five books of the Bible.

If you are a woman who is tied to a religion through your faith and practice weekly, I encourage you to find someone who is like minded and has a personal relationship with the same belief system as you. Or someone who is at least in an active search of a Supreme Being, an entity higher than themselves. This is important because if your belief system and habits are different, he may not be for you. Notice if he only attends service on Easter and Christmas, when/if his favorite sporting team is not playing. Chances are he probably will not change his habits or beliefs simply because you are an active church goer.

Commitment

Commitment is defined as the quality of being dedicated to a cause or person. A purposeful ascension that is supportive, encouraging and deliberate in all aspects of our relationship to each other is what I call commitment. We must be together, passionate about wanting us to win; and intentional about justice and equality for each other and our people.

A healthy commitment is about two people who are willing to adjust, as needed for each other in real time; especially willing to give more when the other can only give less. It is not just where you are in life, but who you have by your side. Having that person who goes through the fire with you is vital for growth to happen.

I enjoy watching professional poker players compete; the stakes are high, and it is thrilling to watch those hands when they "go all in." I have studied their facial expressions, body language and the confidence they exhibit when they "risk it all," the entire pot on a hand.

For me, commitment is like being that poker player; realizing how high the stakes are, and using your intellect, experience and inner knowing that says, "Our relationship is worth it."

Once we get into a space of feeling that a relationship is "right," the pursuit and maintenance of it should be treated as priceless because we believe in each other and are committed to overcoming daily issues together.

It's important to be committed not only to the relationship, but also to the person.

Healing Is a Process

Healing needs to be active, introspective, and honest. Seeking and seeing patterns that have not served you well, especially when those same issues you are complaining about keep showing up. Once a person can realize and acknowledge that "the common denominator is me," and then take responsibility for changing what is not working, the healing process can begin.

When I speak of healing, and I say it is a process, please trust and believe that it is. There are certain issues and/or situations which you may struggle with throughout your lifetime. That is why awareness and acknowledgement are so important. We require an ongoing resolve to get through some situations, especially when it comes to acts of violence, betrayal or loss which can be extremely difficult to heal through. For me, I continue to struggle with the loss of my sister, and how my relationship with her fueled my natural, at times extreme, need to care for others.

My Sister's Keeper

My sister, Rennell, was born with disabilities and had to have open-heart surgery shortly after birth. We were 13 months apart; she was older, but I felt like the big brother. She was smart, beautiful, blue eyed and born blind. We shared a bed until we were seven and six, and continued sharing a bedroom until we got our own rooms around 11 and 10. She was the closest thing to me. Whenever we were out, people would look at her, and I would usually get into a fight or shout, "What are you looking at?" I did not know if they were staring at her blindness or beauty, but I did not care. I internalized it.

For a brief time, my parents separated. During that period, I felt responsible for my sister's care. Once when she was sick, and I heard her coughing in her room. I pretended not to hear her, and my dad reprimanded me for not checking on her. Many times, I felt resentment that she was getting all the attention.

As we got older, I began to admire and respect my sister's bravery and tenacity, though we were not as close because she went to different schools. I started doing my own thing when my parents allowed her to live on campus. For a time, she also lived with our grandmother; and would walk to school, which was about a mile away, by herself. During summer sessions, I would occasionally follow behind, just to be sure she was safe. Every time I saw her making her own way, I was inspired, encouraged, and started appreciating others, especially girls/young women, more.

Around this time, I started hanging out more with women. I missed my sister and I guess their presence filled a bit of the void her daily absence had left. She ended up going to college in Arkansas, getting married and having kids. Because we were so young, I did not get how important it was to communicate regularly. Unfortunately, my sister, whom we never thought would have children, died giving birth to her third child; her heart simply gave out.

There is so much I wanted to tell her, especially how proud I was of her and how strong I thought she was. I used to wish she were not blind; yet, as I matured, I began to appreciate her disability as it enhanced her abilities in other ways. When I was a boy, I shied away from my desire to nurture; as I aged, I began to appreciate it. I miss my sister so much, and though I have prayed, cried, and worked to heal, I still miss her tremendously, and find it difficult to speak about her to this day.

I shared this for several reasons:

1. Each of us come with experiences that have likely been difficult.

2. Trauma and loss affect each person differently; being aware of those effects can support healing, if we are willing to embrace what is happening and try to move through the pain.

3. We can react or be proactive about situations in our lives; and while some things may never "go away," learning to cope and overcome is forward-moving and healthy.

4. Some experiences bring out the best in us in unexpected ways; I believe there are certain natural gifts we are born with that we either gravitate toward or not. It is through living that we get to know ourselves and others, and hopefully learn to do things differently/ better with time and experience.

What does it take to get there?

- Being vulnerable.
- Being honest with yourself, and with others.
- Acknowledgement of what has happened, is happening, and what you'd like to happen going forward.
- Self-love
- Self-respect
- Self-forgiveness

Once you have begun doing your own work, consider how your past actions may have affected others, and be willing to show love, respect and forgiveness to people, in your past, present, and for your future. Healed people often have the desire to see others healed, and once you begin to heal, you will find that it becomes natural to want to support others in doing the same.

Actively investing in your healing is the key. On your path to healing, especially if you have experienced trauma, it can sometimes be made easier with outside resources. This can include reading; participating in group therapy – like grief counseling or appropriate religious groups; and I also recommend therapy. Seeking therapy individually can be extremely helpful; and then participating as a couple, if necessary or desired, can help as well.

Healing is a process and trusting it requires patience, and realizing it is not going to happen overnight. It was practice that created the issue; to change behavior, will take practice as well. Letting go of attachments that do not suit you is important; this may include situations, relationships, or even family members who may impede your healing.

Section Two
The Middle Passage

My years between being young, dumb, and seeking maturity either brought me insight or disappointment because of a few too many wrong turns.

Getting on the right track depends on the amount of perseverance, self-reflection, willingness to learn, and implementing more mature ways of being.

Street Love

Niggah!
You have a lot to learn,
about your sisters.
Your manipulative cool,
your abuse,
not answers.
I saw your love,
a slap,
a kick,
an unwanted dick.
That is machismo.
You Coward!
Kindness is not fashionable?
Brothers why so weak to love,
so strong on dubitation.

41

Mr. Smooth,

I do understand your frustration.

Be kind,

be gentle.

She will make your love strong,

keep pain from your daughters,

bring us sons that belong.

I plea brothers,

change your ways.

Or we will lose something precious,

in the crossover.

– *Randall, 21 years old*

A Dark Age

I had a short phase in my life where my faith wavered in Yahawah, humanity and love. It was the fall of 1989, and it was a dark period for me. It had been the decade of the AIDS and crack epidemics coupled with misogynist music full of "bitches and hoes" lyrics from the minds of popular male hip hop artists. At the height of this period, our people were being shaken emotionally, physically, and spiritually; *and no one was coming to liberate us.*

I was attending an Historically Black College at the time. Going to an HBCU was a unique experience. They constantly encouraged us, building confidence in our blackness, telling us we mattered, which I appreciated. Yet, in this moment, I was sitting in my dorm room contemplating why I was there and what had happened to our people. I was feeling invisible. I began to feel as if I was asphyxiating over lies spread by white propaganda we were being told and "entertained" by; there were too many messages against us, pounding away at the heart and spirit of who we were, who I was, and who I wanted to be. I felt like outside forces were closing in, attempting to keep us bound to their deception.

I needed more than just surface conversations, raunchy music, or random sex. And no, I couldn't even try and "fix" someone else. At that point, I had nothing left to give. I had been spreading pieces of me around and had come up with nothing but hellish, sometimes suicidal thoughts. I just wanted something or someone to breathe life back into me. I needed to know that I was still alive, that I had a chance and a choice, that me and my future actually mattered. I needed peace...

In my search for answers, freedom, and serenity, I started reading the book, *The Cosmic Mother*, by Monica Sjoo & Barbara Mor. I had had the book for a while and was reading it off and on when something hit me. I realized that this disconnect with The Most High I felt was intentional; and I knew I had to figure it out.

I had forgotten what I had been taught about the sanctity of women. I was aware of how Black young men during this time, as a collective were not allies or protectors of women, including me, at times. I had been brought up to respect and honor women yet, we were trapped in the epidemics, ignorantly being swept away, and chained. It made me feel disheartened.

Progressing through the book had me looking at women and the human connection to the world differently than I had before. I saw that we had a responsibility to be truth seekers and to show honor to our Queens and the Black family. I was taught to stand up for women, but now I wanted to invest in their spirits and emotions as a collaborator, not simply as a giver or a taker.

By the time I finished reading the book, I felt hopeful and grounded. I began reconnecting with the Most High on a regular basis and began to experience the freedom and joy that faith brings. As I considered Black women, I wrote the prose "Help Us Black Women" as a message of recognition, change and as an apology.

Help Us Black Women

I live in a lonely world feeling trapped, as if I were nonexistent.

I have tried to figure it out, but it seems I was born without a soul, no true meaning.

There are others that feel as I do.

I imagine we are lost; beings trapped within a closed society.

We were born to die troublesome with no meaning.

They say our history has no beginning and the end is designed as predictable.

It is genocide my sister.

We brothers grow up in the urban jungles of Chicago, Detroit, DC, New York, LA, New Orleans, and St. Louis.

We have learned the truth of nonexistence, a premeditated suffocation of our spirits. Countless appointed role models run by us and offer their wealth of advice.

They say, "Man we are here to rid you of our world."

They run off because they cannot get caught telling the truth. I wonder why?

It is not that I did not understand the message.

I just want to understand why we are so thought of by the messenger.

I hate not knowing, and waiting for each moment to kick me in the ass.

What are my chances?

How long will I live?

Can I afford an opportunity, and is it my blackness that keeps me constantly looking for answers?

We do not seek the cause; only to blame.

What excuses can we offer to show you we are extinct before we are gone?

We are frustrated.

Your love and belief are what we hold on to.

Black women, I am sorry for our ignorance and denial of spiritual virtues.

We want to come home.

Caress our souls and breathe existence through our lungs.

Black women help us!

Hallelujah

Explosion of silky black hair,
elevated to the sky.
Crinkles for every level of care.
Her skin smooth,
self-moisturized.
The first complexion!
Broad shoulders of dignity,
flows through her veins,
pure honesty.
Showing for all womankind.
The quintessence smile,
traces of the Nile,
the Tenacity of Tubman,
the poise of Rosa.
A statue of beauty and strength.

She makes the day seem needed,

an added compliment.

The suns upon her,

a blessing and a friend.

Legs are firm,

showing of a good hard life.

Men gaze and clap in praise.

The pride is in her eyes,

I am hypnotized.

– Randall, 19 years old

Love and Basketball

As a boy, I thought as a boy.

When I thought of being in love, I thought of a warm cathartic feeling inside of my body that brought both a smile and a tear to my face. I beamed because I was happy, and I teared up because I was thankful that someone chose me. After numerous rejections during adolescence, my mind settled into losing confidence and feeling unworthy. My instinct was to stop trying, but I reconsidered because I really thought I was exceptional even if others did not see me. So, I worked hard to be a good listener and learned to read between the lines in conversation; just like I read the defense on a basketball court to get the ball to my player for the championship game-winning shot.

As a kid, I loved pick-up basketball, but I did not get picked for the first game most of the time because of the risk; the risk of not being good enough. And, truthfully, I did not like the feeling it gave me. I mean who would? I wanted to be desirable and to be "picked first," so I worked hard on my game. I was quick, so stealing the ball came easily, and I loved sharing the "roc," which is what ballers call the basketball. I also started shooting with both hands, which made me more competitive and more likely to make points. Of course, other players knowing this would choose me just on that alone. My style was complimentary, so they knew I would make them look good, and I wouldn't hog the ball.

When it came to dating, rejection was exceedingly difficult to face, as we are told that it is all on us, the male, to ask, for the number or the date; however, I do not think most women understood how difficult it was to ask. After a few girls saying, "No, I don't want to dance," or "No, I have a boyfriend," it makes us apprehensive about asking, like being last picked for a game. It messes with our esteem.

Changing the Results

Eventually on the basketball court, I was getting picked first, and being selected was a confidence builder. It also made me lazy because, after a while, I would just get picked based on my reputation, and not what I could truly offer the team, in any given moment. Granted, I had already done the work that got me noticed, but if I am being honest, sometimes I was not worthy of being chosen on that day. I was just going through the motions, like I would sometimes do in my relationships as I aged.

So, as an adolescent, just like when I deliberately set out to improve and build my skills in basketball, I intentionally set out to learn more about women. I decided to read magazines, to get to the source. In *Cosmo*, a popular women's magazine at the time, there were many articles about women's emotions, which were insightful, as I tried to relate to what girls were saying. I read *Playboy* magazine too; in addition to the beautiful pictures, they had great articles, especially those that dealt with the sexual desires of a woman, and how to please. Of course, I enjoyed this new-found knowledge and could not wait to practice.

I wanted to transform myself into the hero of the love songs of my favorite musical artists. Their songs would eventually turn into the soundtracks of my post-adolescent romantic life. They were a measuring stick for how I wanted to love and be loved for always and forever; grateful to Luther Vandross for showing me it was okay to acknowledge my own emotions.

Beyond Games

My favorite poet, Kahlil Gibran writes, "Between what is said and not meant, and what is meant and not said, most of love is lost." What does this mean? We often do not have the words to speak into someone, and sometimes the words we do have cause us pain and confusion. But, when we can focus on what is important, like, communication, commitment, and Spirit, we can get what we need.

Sankofa Love is that journey into transparency that results in us both becoming winners, because we have each other!

Like basketball, being a winner in love often comes with rejections before that special one sees you, and you, together, become a winning team. Your potential partner does not know your skill set, your style, nor your level of commitment. Different skills are required to be chosen for the long-haul; the 'til death do us part choosing. Being a future spouse is a one-on-one sport; and, being chosen and sustained is more complicated; it takes hard work. We as men love women, and we often love sports because both are mysterious; both represent the unknown, the possibilities, and the opportunities. It is the stimuli of not knowing what is going to happen, yet working toward a common objective that is rewarding, satisfying, and even thrilling, despite the outcome.

Once I truly, deeply realized why Yahawah created love, that we are each created to love and be loved, in return, I knew then that my purpose was to act out this directive to seek love for myself, like LL Cool J, "I need love."

My master plan was this: the more women seeing my truth in action, hearing my vulnerability in words, noticing me, the greater chance I had at being chosen; so, I began working toward that end.

I learned that women wanted to see our actions, not our words. I had to be noticed, and talked about for a wonderful woman to take a risk on choosing me for her team. I believed the moment I was chosen, she would become my teammate, partner and hopefully, we would become a winning combination. I would be her star player and cheerleader; through sharing, protecting, encouraging and being present to assist her and us. I wanted to share the championship with the goal of both being winners. I was learning that to create a winning team takes sacrifice, practice, tenacity, focus, and perseverance. I was beginning to recognize which skills needed to be built, while maintaining patience and passion.

I was once involved with a beautiful, vivacious woman who had my heart. I wanted to dream with her, and I wanted her to succeed beyond her wildest imagination. She was brilliant and a successful entrepreneur; however, she was not a people person; she was reserved and had a difficult time opening up and showing her personality in work situations. I became her personal public relations corner man. It was easy for me because I believed in her and wanted her to shine. As we attended luncheons, meetings, and gatherings, I made it my business to share her accomplishments, successes, and talents, thus making it easier for her to form better connections and to accomplish her business goals. For a moment we became that winning combination; however, the passion and patience were not enough to sustain our journey together.

In basketball, the goal is for the team to win the game, the season and ultimately to become champions. In love and partnership, the goal is to communicate, commit, come together and ultimately become lifelong partners and companions. I deserve to be picked and so do you.

Encouragement is a gift, and your partner should always know that you are her/his number one fan.

Beware of Patterns that May Undermine Relationships

Most of my closest friends are women, which for the most part has been positive; however, having them so close, also caused conflict and insecurity with some of the women I dated. Despite my loyalty to my woman, I learned that you should not be so readily available to another woman no matter the friendship, once you are in an intimate relationship. I had to adapt to be more considerate and validate my woman's feelings regardless of my words of affirmation that they were the only one.

I can honestly say that it was difficult because I was fine with my woman having male friends, especially if she was honest, and they were a part of her life before I entered it. I believe that you trust a person until they give you a reason not to. From talking to my women friends I learned how women think, feel, and typically operate. Sometimes they did not always articulate their true feelings for fear of conflict. Not only were these conversations valuable, but also seeing, first-hand what challenges women face regularly helped me to be more sensitive and supportive.

A person's wounds can become a collage of events tracing back to childhood trauma, misinformation, projections, or blame. Dysfunctional home life has created generational family issues that become exacerbated by absentee parents, lack of daddy's affection, not being good enough in mom's eyes, and episodes of abuse from physical and emotional to sexual. When girls do not get daddy's attention or affection, they often seek it in immature relationships with boys, not knowing it is dysfunctional. When boys do not get attention or affection from their dad's, they often get bitter toward women because they do not know how to treat them – and often become angry. In order to get his "manhood," he thinks smashing a woman will bring it to him. There is a difference between manhood and males. Faulty patterns of needs versus wants, and any other number of factors contribute to this unhealthy bond.

Pay Attention to Manipulation

In basketball, we force the opponent to the side he leans on the most to steal the ball. Once that happens, we have an advantage. It makes one familiar with the defensive stance of the opponent, and we then use that knowledge to create our strategy to conquer and win. Reading the defense of a woman is figuring out what she leans on more than anything: Is it her looks, money, possessions, career, or body? Or, we notice that she is an "independent woman" who says that she doesn't need a man. Whatever the opportunity, there are strategies that men use to break down a woman's defense to get to her. When women hold onto certain external attributes; men can use them as a way in to establish influence; because we know you are comfortable dribbling on that one side and will say it works for you until the ball, or in this case, your heart gets stolen.

Speaking as a man, some of us are broken.

We tend to lean on the fact that we know there are more women than men, thus the notion we have more options. That means we don't have to work hard for the courtship. Additionally, we may have the superficial attention grabber of a nice car, lofty income, swag, good-looks, body and/or the reputation of being a good lover. However, we may not be "assisting" in her tranquility in our ego game of pursuit.

It's important to know who you are, what you stand for and where you are in your life's journey before you attach yourself to another person because external attractions or emotional entanglements will further complicate life; especially if you haven't healed from past trauma. When you are in a healthy space, you can be a partner, and it is much more difficult for a person to manipulate you.

Create Partnership

Healthy relationships need balance, cooperation, and common goals. When a potential mate is loving and open, they are supportive, communicative and they encourage their partner to express her/himself, without judgment or punishment. True teammates/partners will feel responsibility toward the other, resulting in mutual trust and respect in their shared journey. When we are open and work to understand, we realize that the only thing we should be leaning on is our authenticity; designed before we were born.

Getting Uncomfortable

Vulnerability, after healing from trauma can even be sexy, if we can get to it. Men are not taught to be vulnerable, it is considered to not be manly; yet, I realize now, over the age of 50, that no one is perfect, especially me. However, if I expect her to open up, I must first take the lead – someone has to, if we are to be one, together. The world is full of lonely lovers waiting for someone to make the first move. Being vulnerable builds trust, resolves conflict and opens up communication.

Many men do not know how to seek love unselfishly, and after they become burned or wounded, refuse to take risks necessary to create true partnership. When we do not take risks, we miss the opportunity of freedom, surrendering and joy to be found in our life saver/help mate/destined love.

Both genders are guilty of trying to control their relationships based on superficial lists filled with things they think matter, resulting in fantasies, disappointment, or malnourished love. Unfortunately, there are many lonely people wanting to be loved, but because they are not risk takers willing to go beyond their threshold or comfort zones, they remain unfulfilled and single.

For example, an entrepreneur who takes a risk on a business with a partner, by putting money up, is "putting skin in the game." Because of this, the partner knows they are committed. The risk includes potentially losing the investment to gain dividends, resulting in profit. Relationships are similar; take the risk, create a healthy life and family, and enjoy the gains of a fulfilling, solid love.

We as lovers must learn how to trust each other at some point by taking risks, especially men. Love does not want us to be like the Hebrew children of Egypt who wanted to return to slavery because of the unknown. A man should be worthy of following because of his love for a woman in both his words and actions. Love wants men to step out of their comfort zones like Abraham of the Bible. Love asks us to be brave, to sacrifice, to commit, to trust and to *compromise* for rewards unknown to us now. You cannot make a person ready for what you are ready for, and you should not wait around for them to make up their mind. If you cannot do that, you are not READY!

Wet Dreams

A smile of beauty,

innocently portrayed

the sun set, thoughts rise,

as I lay.

Bless be my heart,

as my thoughts are pure.

I have symptoms of you,

you are my cure.

Wanting you in so many ways,

creating a situation,

can't be delayed.

Yet, I do need you,

the selfishness I have.

We must not depart as we are,

You are a part of my path.

I desperately think,

the next time we sleep.

Wondering each day,

my images are incomplete.

If love is what I am after,

it is you I want to feel the laughter.

Sorry for all the dreams,

promises to you.

Wanted to keep you near,

always true.

If I had it to do again,

never would my values bend.

A disgrace I must seem.

Give me another chance,

I will bring reality from a dream.

– Randall, 23 years old

From Across the Room

Prior to marriage, I had a type. Like many of my romantic
stories, it was always a woman across the crowded room,
followed by my wanting to rescue her. I would see
something of my parents or my sister in her, and I thought
'I had to have her'. We all have patterns we continue
to let fester until we do not.

While in college, she was a hard sistah from up north.
A ten-foot invisible wall surrounded her every move. I
followed her, looking to break that wall down and grovel
before her physical beauty. I knew she had tears and
would feel compassion for my wretched soul. It appeared
she wanted men to be intimidated.

I might have been young, but I was an old fashioned
brother. I understood my resilient virtues. I had been
looking for my soul mate for what seemed to be a long
time; I was not going to let her repression smother me.

I thought. *She is the perfect one for me.*

I saw my mother's warmth and love, my father's fighting instinct and common sense, and my sister's naiveté and tenacity. She was already a part of me, and I did not even know her name. I wanted her, and all she possessed. She was lonely and afraid.

I thought. *She is the perfect one for me.*

The problem was climbing over that damn wall, so she could kiss my lonesome heart. I was determined. She was not aware of her strength and jurisdiction over men. I was aware, and I wanted her as my queen. It was obvious to me, she had a past that had seen its share of heartaches. I had to prove myself worthy.

I thought. *She is the perfect one for me.*

This was not the first time I thought I had found my mate. You see, I thought I had found love, and many times pretended I knew love. I looked at her, and I was *in love.*

All I needed now was to hear her say she could love me, forever, always.

I thought. *She is the perfect one for me.*

I wanted to hold her and render security, comfort, trust and love.

I thought. *She is the perfect one for me.*

I was scared, but only at the chance of losing her. It was my chance to make us happy.

I thought. She *is the perfect one for me.*

Wish me luck AGAIN!

I wasn't ready… but I was close…

Love must be centered on acceptance and not unnecessary expectations.

We should decide early on what we will comfortably accept, because it probably won't change. And if you are expecting something different than what was presented, you are doing yourself a disservice.

I extended myself so many times to become only a friend with emotional benefits, while *she* held out, waiting for her imaginary and delusional expectations to materialize which did me a disservice each time.

We all want to be chosen. It was Robert Frost who said, "Love is an irresistible desire to be irresistibly desired." Unrequited love is not love because it is not reciprocal. The greatest form of love is acceptance of a person, including flaws.

Section Three
Seven Stories

Inspired by my Facebook posts...

The Days

*"Until the end of time, I'll be there for you. You own
my heart and mind, I truly adore you."* – Prince

Facebook Posting, Day One: *"From the moment I decided
that I wanted to find a partner, I wanted her, even before we met,
to have amazing days."*

"I hope you're having an amazing day." #onelove

*They say every day is a new day. There are 12 hours in a
complete day, and I want the day to count and not just count
them waiting on time to decide. We are the masters of our
days. I want you to know, I am going to make a conscientious
effort to spend at least six of those hours (the number six
being both perfect and harmonious), showing you adoration
with my words and actions until the end of time. I am not sure
if that is what Prince was saying in his song, but it is my
intention. We can decide what kind of day we want to have.*

We can choose to be happy, adventurous, majestic, silly, or serious. I want to make your day; I want to wake up next to you. Period!

I thought I could be responsible for someone else's happiness. I thought that because I had worked on myself, I was also ready to live an amazing life. I imagined someone coming into my space who wanted to add to it, build on it, and create from it. All I wanted was for her to have an amazing day, an amazing life, and I wanted nothing in return, but to see her happy. It is a difficult task to be responsible for someone's happiness. I have seen too many lovers try to take on that responsibility and fail miserably every time. It is actually impossible. However, remnants of when I was younger, I thought that is what it meant to be a committed lover.

When I was in college, I had a stranger tell me his idea of happiness in a relationship; this happened during an unprompted conversation while on my lunch break in Piedmont Park in Downtown Atlanta. I remember having a lot on my mind; mostly about the young lady I was living with at the time. I did not exactly welcome his words or his invasion of my space or thoughts. I did not give him that "familiar nod" that gave him permission to continue. I feel like he ignored my body language; it was as if he needed to tell me, and I needed to listen.

He wore long locs and soiled clothes, appearing to be homeless. Yet, when he spoke there was depth and wisdom that flowed through his spirit. I remember looking up at him and feeling less irritable and more peaceful. He seemed to pierce my soul with his eyes while acknowledging my sadness through his expression. That caught me off guard. I had been contemplating suicide around that time, and I was thrown off balance with this strange, invasive, yet caring interaction. Naturally, I wanted to throw him off track and get him out of my soul; so, I gave him that Randall smile.

I have a smile that tends to put others at ease when I am at a low. He sensed my betrayal of myself and began to speak like we were already immersed in a conversation. He told me that happiness equaled a dollar. He said that each person must have 50 cents worth of their own happiness that they can bring to a relationship. Therefore, if your partner has 35 cents and you have your 50 cents, there is nothing you can do to get to that dollar.

He continued, "Your instinct is to help your partner, but whatever you give takes away from your 50 cents. They must find 15 more cents to have their own happiness before you can have a dollar's worth of happiness together."

It took me a long time to process that wisdom. What I concluded was that I am not responsible for anyone's happiness but mine; and though I can say it, changing patterns would not be easy. It is ironic that eleven years later, I would be homeless, going through a divorce with long flowing locs connecting with the soul of a young man who was headed down the wrong path. We must realize that our journeys connect us all to one another.

**Though I am not "in charge" of your happiness;
I would like to be a willing participant in
creating joy, together.**

Let's be present every single day; let's take time and be intentional to share our thoughts, feelings and concerns; let's protect each other and provide comfort, stimulation and serenity. There are things we can enjoy...

I genuinely want to wake up next to you and cherish my highest form of love that makes you feel it is right to be safe and protected in my arms. The time is never ever right until you know it is right. Do not be afraid to be loved because I will not enter you under false pretense, but from a space of integrity of mirrored words to actions. I only ask that you let me love you, and I promise, while holding your heart in my hands, I vow not to drop it.

Each new day presents an opportunity to be grateful. We can share our first moments in meditation, filled with deep breathing, acknowledging, and thanking The Most

High for His downloads. Experiencing shared breathing provides an energetic force and brings us to oneness. **Every day is a new day.**

We can enjoy pillow talks before our "grand rising" or even before bed-sharing our intimate times and gathering our thoughts, creating a sanctuary of connection, enlightenment, and new opportunities. This clarity is necessary for our survival in a world where others can consciously and subconsciously try to disrupt our mission. **Every day is a new day**.

Realizing that old habits and patterns may need to change, we make a commitment together to shred all dysfunction and misinformation; admitting to our flaws and working to do and be better. One cannot take back words; it is like trying to put toothpaste back into the tube. It is messy and impossible. Therefore, as we experience our new days, we commit to embracing the power in our thoughts, and the words we speak; mindful of the seeds we plant. We think and share words of affirmation and adoration throughout the day; and we do our best to speak truth and to be in integrity even during difficult conversations. As we complete the day, we appreciate the lessons and experiences, allowing them to be in the rear view, as we continue ahead, seizing on the present moment and looking toward what is next. We choose not to go to bed angry, judgmental, resentful or without being honest that something is happening. We choose to be hopeful, wise, and gentle with one another. We give these gifts of love and accountability to one another with the expectation that our communication must be honest for us to grow. **Every day is a new day.**

"You're my morning star shining brightly beside me, And if we keep this love, We will last through all eternity." – Natalie Cole

I Wash Dishes

"You don't have to... look no... Don't have to look no further
cuz I am right before ya with me... things will be...better
cuz I'm not here to hurt ya I'm just here to love ya."
– Carl Thomas

Vulnerability, humility, and leadership can and do go together, though most women may or may not recognize or appreciate those traits in a supportive, strong partner.

Facebook Posting, Day Two: *"I am a husband who prays for my wife. Leads her boldly. Serves her humbly. And cherishes her deeply."*

While at a bar in L.A., I was eavesdropping on a conversation where an attractive woman was talking about what kind of man she wanted. He had to be an, "Alpha male, with a six-figure income and tall." As she postured with a grimace, held her arms like she was doing a B-Boy stance, and shared her version of swag, I took note. She giggled right after her comment and followed up with nothing else.

I thought, "That's interesting; she's leaving so many traits and characteristics out."

Alpha, defined, refers to the dominance of an animal, or leader of the pack. Yet, there's more than aggression and dominance to manhood. Women have the power to get different results. However, if a woman does not recognize or acknowledge the power and the way she deserves to be treated, we continue to live in cycles of dysfunction. We don't understand what affects our women, affects our nation. My dad would always say, "You train a person how to treat you." Well, we must remember that, especially when imagining our ideal mate, and what we deem as important.

We must come to grips with what it means to "be a man" and not let stereotypes direct us.

At his core, a worthy man is not just his appearance or bank account. Consider, too, he should be stable, ambitious, passionate. And, what of his character? His disposition? His sense of purpose and direction? He should be focused, intellectually and spiritually curious, insightful, aware of his history and confident. He should exhibit humility, courage, and a forgiving spirit; these are traits that define a man.

If we allowed that woman in the bar to define us, we would be limited in countless ways. Many men would get passed over not only because of their aesthetics, but because they do not fit the stereotype that is often dreamed about while flipping through Instagram.

Alpha man or superior man? Gentle can also be an expression of strength, especially as it comes to interacting with our Queens. In order to be successful, leadership can be found in flexibility and strength, guidance and listening, going first and falling back all traits of manhood, in maturity. In chaos and disorder, in spotlight or behind the curtain, in the boardroom or in the kitchen; true men know how to compromise and sacrifice.

I love to see others shine and be their best. I have always thought of myself as a piece of the many puzzles I come across and being the missing piece for completion. It is more powerful to know that you can depend on someone, who when he says he got you, he got you. It will free you up to be your best, and that is my desire. We are on the same team. I am not your competitor.

You are unique, intelligent, amazing, talented, stunning, and most importantly, a gift from The Most High.

As I have matured and observed many relationships, both my own and others, I know many women today are exhibiting more as "alpha women," having to lean on their more masculine vibrations. This often happens because of having to work and raise a family on their own, without assistance; and upon finding a male, he may be either too weak or too domineering- disguising himself as a man.

A real man respects and recognizes a woman's strength and protects her when she is depleted, or is feeling unsupported. The weak male tries to capitalize on the side she is leaning on, like body, beauty, bank account or accomplishments.

I admit I am turned on by a strong woman who still embraces her feminine vibration. My mom is one, and I admire her for it; yet, both of my parents have strong personalities. She does not act like an "alpha woman" with my dad.

My mom was the first woman chief of her department, where hundreds of her employees were men. My father was a highly respected professional in the restaurant industry who was adept at dealing with the men of industry he encountered daily; those he influenced, and those he encountered in the streets.

My dad was never the loudest one in the room, but he always commanded authority. His presence, confidence and reputation naturally earn respect when he enters a room. He recognized that his wife needed more affection and attention than other women because of her job, and he made it his business to give it to her. A true man to the core, he also cooked, and was the voice of reason when chaos erupted during family tragedies which is certainly necessary for black families in urban environments.

I See You

I see the sensitive side that makes up the woman in you. I will be strong while taking care of your needs without making you feel like I am handling you.

I'm gonna make it alright.

I will cover your front and your back.

I am here to protect you, to lead you and to provide the strength you need, so that you have the balance you deserve.

I'm gonna make it alright.

It is my honor to speak life into you, spiritually speaking. I edify you, treat you with love and respect; and hope that we do that mutually.

I'm gonna make it alright.

I know you are capable of many and perhaps even all things, yet, I need you to allow me to fall on the sword when it comes to you and to us.

I need you to trust me.

I'm gonna make it alright.

I need you to let that ten-foot invisible wall in front of you crumble because I am going to need you to breathe life back into me as well.

Me, being a real Black man, does not mean I do not need your strength Queen; I will be inspired by your tenacity, and delighted by your presence.

I love and commit to you.

I'm gonna make it alright.

Ego-tripping

Life's only true orgasm,
exist above the waist,
between the ears.
Riding along the currents,
the supernatural.
Not knowing if the waters are
bitter or sweet.
If it's magical,
or observationally spiritual.
It's not the taste that matters,
it's the wetness.

To lay in it,

jack-off in it,

allowing the vile,

traveling downstream,

water falling into,

a wine glass.

Served chilled to the one you adore.

– Randall, Age 25

Agape,
Unconditional Love

"And we'll always be together, our love. My love is surely one thing you can surely depend on in times of darkness and fear, I go to you; I know you'll make me strong.

You're gonna make me happy.
You're gonna make me smile." – Natalie Cole

Facebook Posting, Day Three: *"Every day I will tell you I love you and mean it, even when you haven't eaten that day, or are on your menstrual, having hormone issues or you start snapping on me."*

The first time I met Natalie Cole was at One Church in LA. I escorted her to her seat and told her I loved her. With no hesitation, she kissed me on the cheek. Somehow, I think she knew I was that 13-year-old kid who started listening to her albums and fell in love with her soulful description of how love should be. Months later, she would be gone, but her songs forever would live in my soul. I wanted my love to be everything she described; and why not?

Who does not want an "inseparable" love; that "true love" that takes your heart and runs with it? Well, the problem is and always will be the baggage that comes with being "in love," and unfortunately, we all have it. Relationships thrive when you can drop off that old luggage once you arrive at your destination. The idea is to release the past and move forward with no regrets and with someone who has chosen to help you unpack the baggage. I believe too many of us let our damaged hearts and scars stay damaged and unhealed because we don't get loved the way we thought we should, thus keeping us from the one that is willing to love you unconditionally, and who will always be around despite your baggage and his own to assist in the healing.

I am not captain-save-a-woman. However, I will do my best to validate and simply listen. I will also offer suggestions; only if that is your desire. I know you have been independent, so I will not give up on us just because you are in a certain mood. I will not participate in patterns of self-sabotage because of fear or miscommunication. My ego is not so fragile that I will retreat if you get into a certain mood and feel the need to emasculate me if you feel vulnerable, especially about your independence.

We all have insecurities, including me. It is those insecurities along with your strengths, desires, and compassion that make you the phenomenal woman that you are. Queen never forget that you are a life giver; not just someone's lost rib to be found.

Men who are emotionally unavailable often play on women's past relationships, self-doubt, and feelings. In the movie *Baby Boy*, Jody throws the insecurity ploy in Yvette's face when he is caught sleeping around. He invalidates her love and affection, disrespects her, and then blames her; and somehow, he frames everything to be her fault. It was not. Some males, like Jody's character, are too lazy or scared, to look inward and fight off those inner demons that lurk in the ravages of an absentee father experience, coddling mother, or unstable childhood.

I have seen so many "baby boys" who define manhood by the number of women they smash, needing sex with multiple women to feel secure; that's one of the reasons they don't mature and become men. We as males, often have double standards, and they affect the way we act. However, I will not complain or leave you just because you pass gas in the middle of the night. I am grateful that my dad validated my manhood, teaching me characteristics and habits, giving examples and guidance on how to respect and treat women. I have done and continue to do the work.

As we are authentic and honest with ourselves, evolving, we become ready for what is next. Nathaniel Hawthorne, an American novelist known for his dark romanticism said, *"No man, for any considerable period, can wear one face to himself, and another to the multitude, without finally getting bewildered as to which may be the truth."*

Keepin' It Righteous vs. Real

When we first start dating someone, we tend to put on our "best face"- not necessarily our "true face." Let us keep it *"righteous"* and forego the *"real"* part, because nowadays most would not know what is real if it was smack dab in our faces. You see, Jody *was keepin' it real* when he said he would not sleep with a girl at Yvette's job because of "the code" since they worked together. Negro please. He did not say he would not cheat; he just said he would not cheat with someone at Yvette's job; and then he did! Jody thought that being "honest" and justifying his infidelity, he was *keepin' it real*; that was not righteous. And, she kept letting him come back.

"Phantom pain" is a term used to describe the sensation soldiers might have as if a limb is still attached after amputation; so much that they would even reach for it like it is still a part of his/her body. Like Yvette, many of us continue to stay in or invite pain back into our lives. Doing this is like experiencing phantom pain. It lives with us until it does not; until we decide to do something about it, training ourselves, repeatedly, recognizing that it is no longer there, accepting reality; we continue.

Regarding the phantom phenomenon, I know what it is like to hold on to something that is gone. I did that for a while when I cut off my locs after 15 years; grabbing for them, though they were not there. It took about six months for me to truly release them.

Humans carry patterns with them formed from past relationships, habits, feelings, emotions and especially pain. And, although the situation(s) may have past, the sensation remains. However, making righteous choices means recognizing what has happened, and seeking an inner solution instead of normalizing, "keeping it real."

It is important that we do our work, providing our own self-acknowledgement and oxygen masks, and being free from phantom pain before attempting to enter into a new, healthy relationship. I am also speaking to the men who are accustomed to trying to be the "captain" feeling as if we must try and save our mate, or vice versa. Once each of us takes responsibility for ourselves and becomes properly positioned for love, we can take care of one another in our own unique ways, because we have enough to give and to share.

When men and women come together, women often expand the vision and life of a properly positioned man, though she may have not been taught that she carries that vision. The man may not have been taught to receive it.

However, part of a woman's power is igniting what is inside the man who is ready for her. When the man finds himself awakening, the dormancy eased, righteous living and real love can bring out the best in the man, and the woman, his Queen.

A One Woman Man

Unlike 'Baby Boy' who was not mature enough to understand that one whole woman is enough for one whole man, men should choose to be a one-woman man. Scripture declares, "You seek, and you shall find, knock and the door will be opened and answered." (Matt 7:7) Therefore, each man has a choice to decree and declare:

> *Queen, I assure you, my expression and commitment to your way of love is a priority to me. I will ask questions when I do not understand. I will share openly and be honest when asked questions by you. I choose to accept who you are. I will not take things personally, and I will listen to what you are actually sharing with me. I will always knock on your door and seek only your fulfillment; no one else's. I will be straightforward with my intentions and do my best to keep your love tank full until death do us part, upon our marriage. I will always choose you; simply because I vow to love you*

unconditionally. I am blessed to have found you, who makes me feel like no other. To quote Dave Hollister, who says it best, to be "Blessed to find that one who makes 'you' feel like no other," is my declaration.

I will always come home to you.

I Got You

"It's so good lovin' somebody, and that somebody loves you back.

To be loved and be loved in return; it's the only thing that my heart desires." – Teddy Pendergrass

Facebook Post, Day Four: *"Our journey is not going to be perfect, but I will stick with us 'til the very end. I will protect your heart. And, I will love you madly; I got you."*

When I was a kid, I saw the womenfolk make plates of food for their spouses/partners at every family function. My mom did this for my dad. I thought it was their womanly duty. It wasn't until I got older that I realized this practice of making plates evolved out of love and respect for their Kings from these Queens who were holding it down in the home.

They knew their Kings needed to be built up due to the things they had to endure as black men in the world, outside the home. It was the least they could do for them to make them feel special, and like men.

As I matured my primary love language changed from *Quality Time* to *Acts of Service*. I remember once dating someone, and she and I were out to lunch. I ordered for us. It was family style, and the moment the food arrived, she started making my plate. I wanted to love her right there at that moment! It was the hottest thing ever. That meant so much to me, I could not wait to reciprocate the gesture. I told her in that moment, "Whatever you want, I got it."

The vibration I had when I said, "I got you," had more intention behind it than me saying, "I love you." I love everybody, but it does not imply, "I got you."

My statement meant:

I am going to take care of you, and you can depend on that because I got you.
Having your back will show up in my responsibility and behavior when I got you.
Whenever you need me, I got you.

We are all connected and must be cautious about our vibration. Everything is about vibration. If every time I am around you, you leave me with mixed feelings, uncertainty, or an unsettled spirit, I am not placing my vibration with you. The way I feel around you determines my connection to you.

You can tell a lot about a person by the way they hug you. Hugging is a powerful connection to healing sickness, disease, depression, anxiety, and loneliness. I love to hug. A hug can instantly boost Oxytocin levels, which restore feelings of connectedness. I love to hug for a period because I know that an extended time lifts one's serotonin levels, elevating mood and creating happiness.

Our hugs and our love start and end with intention. You see, there are going to be times in our life when a good, long hug is all that is needed.

I Am Your King

The scriptures talk about showing honor to women as the weaker vessel, since they are heirs with us, so that our prayers may not be hindered. Too many women get caught up in the "weaker" part and not the joint "heir" or "honor." In the game of chess, the most powerful piece is the queen. In the biggest box office superhero movie of all times, The Black Panther, Chadwick Boseman, King T'Challa, is surrounded by women soldiers led by his female General Okoye who fights for him and their kingdom with strength and integrity, despite not having his superpower. She fights with her heart, talents, commitment, and loyalty.

Before the present day's muscular and athletic football quarterbacks, past legends were not the most athletic and strongest players on the team. Quite the contrary, they were protected by the stronger players. Back then some might have called the quarterbacks the weaker vessel, but they commanded authority and were instrumental in advancing down the field to score touchdowns, using every offensive player at their disposal. Champion teams won with everyone contributing, not just the quarterback, despite him not being the physically strongest guy on the field.

Any man who recognizes the strength and power of the Queen/woman, knows it is his obligation and duty to show up; get his blessings, save the kingdom, and win the championship. This man also knows his woman is there for him, and he must be there for her through it all, the good, bad, and ugly.

I was speaking to a friend one day about the word "help-mate," and how it relates to the scriptures, and its often misrepresentation. The translation does a disservice to women and the placement of their true purpose in the marital union. The Hebrew translation "ezer kenegdo," means "life-saver." In other words, the woman's active, loving, and attentive presence is the lifeline of the relationship.

We talked about our past relationships, and that not all women are groomed to be life savers. They may be good on paper, but ill-prepared or resistant to making a plate at the family gatherings, or supporting her man when he is losing his way. Men need encouragement and support as well.

My friend went on to tell me the story of when he was mowing his and his neighbor's lawn on a hot, humid summer's day. Not one time did his now former spouse offer him a cold drink. As he recalled the story, I could hear the pain in his voice. Knowing he was not supported hurt deeply, and although his wife believed him to be "the one for her," he recognized she was not, and could not be that for him. It was not in her.

When a woman uplifts her man, she makes them greater together.

When a man lovingly respects his woman, he makes them powerful together.

As much as I got you, it must be reciprocal for this to work.

To my future wife I say, "I know there will be times when you feel you must go it alone. I promise not to take it personally. I will give you time to focus on your needs and desires; I'll still be present. I got you."

We have got to have the space, freedom, and opportunity to communicate with each other without being judged or confined by others in our lives.

I got you.

Passion Fruit
of Marital Bliss

teeth/biting

pinkie finger

lickin'

teeth/piercing

velvet wetness

drippin'

tongue/shouting

stem nipples

oval navel

swimming across

into

heavenly bliss

teeth/clenching

nose pressing

breath hot

from a captivated sucking

to a smile

of saliva lips

for a sweet

sugary kiss.

– Randall, Age 26

Speaking in Tongues

*"You should let me love you. Let me be the one to give
you everything you want and need,
baby good love and protection." –* Mario

Facebook Post, Day Five: *"I patiently await the arrival of
you, in anticipation of our exploration of both the world and one
another; I want to be with you and only you. As our journeys
unfold in hotel rooms and scenic balconies around the world,
so will the depth of my passion, erupting like quakes in your
legs with screams of my name from your lips. I will forever
speak life into your soul at sunset, and I will start anew at
sunrise."*

As a species, we have been robbed of our authenticity
by a trapped mind-set. We must never forget we are
considered children of the sun. Our spiritual nature is fed
by energy from the sun as our melanin soaks up its rays.
Relationships solely based on sexual vibration will not fare
well in the long-term; when the physical aspects fade, so

does the love. But if our energy consumption is harnessed, our love lasts "til the end of time."

Grandmother's Wisdom

When I was about to turn thirteen, that rite of passage into adulthood, Grandma Mattie Mason sat me down and asked, "Has your dad had the sex talk with you?"

"Yes, Ma."

She smiled and said, "Okay, then let me tell you a story about vibration."

Turns out it was just another version of the sex talk. She said men have a powerful vibrational force that, when released, can produce life or death into a receptacle. At that age, I did not know what a receptacle was.

She proceeded to tell me that the receptacle, when it receives this vibration, depending on the intent, can make a gray day sunny or a sunny day hot as hell. I did not have a clue what she was saying.

I nodded my head in the affirmative and smiled that smile I inherited from her as she proceeded to tell me that the more this vibrational force goes out into multiple receptacles, the less vibration it retains, and that soon it loses all its power and identity.

"Do you understand?" At first, I nodded my head in the affirmative and then, because I felt bad lying, I said, "No."

She said, "That's okay, you will."

My grandmother planted a seed of wisdom in me which saved me from death on many occasions. It was not until 10 years later that I fully understood what she was saying.

The life force that an orgasm has, with all its DNA, memories, and intentions, should be reserved for the person worthy of all that which is sacred. I soon realized that sexual vibration guides us into a holistic spiritual energy, which leads to creating purpose within that desired oneness with a partner.

One of the tricks of the Evil One is convincing men their manhood validation comes from how they conquer the life source, and how many bottoms they can hit. Swish!

As a young adult male, I wanted to please a woman sexually and felt bad when I thought I did not. I also had this "savior" mentality and through reading those magazines at the time, I soon found out many women do not have orgasms. That truly broke my heart.

After studying about orgasms and vibration because of grandma's wisdom, I realized that orgasms harnessed the right way, produce rejuvenating power, creativity and in some cases, telepathy. Seriously.

Before I was married, making love became an art form to me, but I could not do it with multiple women. You see, when grandma was talking about losing yourself, she was talking about those guys smashing it with any and everybody. They were releasing so much of who they were into this one and that one, that they lost their identity. Thinking sex is all that is needed and wanted causes one to be lost, period.

When one is acting the part of a player, his true purpose and destiny is being played and drained. He, in turn, provides the seed for the bitter, angry woman to grow. And, the woman who allowed this drained soul, a stranger to sleep with her, may have been thinking all the while the sex was going to make him care.

Loving Your Naked Soul

Before I see your naked body, I must connect with your naked soul, and our soul vibration makes me worthy of connecting to your naked body. My intentions are to deposit life, not death, into your portal, to make your gray days sunny, but not unbearably hot. Like Joe sang, "I want to know what turns you on, so I can be all that and more." Because, at the end of the day, *I really want you to let me love you.*

If we are to evolve consciously as one, we must always go to the source. Contrary to Western thought, our orgasm will help raise our consciousness into a loving partnership. When grandma was telling me about this vibration, which is a life force, she said the more you release it into multiple receptacles, the closer to death (spiritual, emotional, and sometimes physical), it brings you. However, I am talking about spiritual death, the loss of identity and purpose. I want us to have healthy orgasms together. I love yoga for this purpose. Meditation/prayer is something I want to encourage you and us to be active in. I want us to seek quiet time, so that we learn to harness this energy that will circulate a soul tie so strong that looking at one another will bring on an orgasm. I am just saying. All things are possible through prayer.

My Queen, the intention when we make love on our wedding day will be built on the understanding that our orgasms will open the higher chakras and create a process of enlightenment into a higher consciousness. Yes, seriously.

So, are you thinking, "How does this happen?" Let me tell you...

It starts with meditation. Temple love! We pray as a way of speaking to The Most High who created us. We ask for the things we desire. If sex was created by Yahawah, I say pray for that sexual connection that was created for pleasure, so that we have all of what Spirit wills us to have. Beloved, this may sound a little unorthodox, but praying before we make love with the intention of growing with each other, will create a satisfying sexual relationship. *You should let me love you.*

Our commitment does not start with our outer appearance or what our bodies look like under our clothes though outside stimulation can serve as mental foreplay. Our sexual vibration begins with the spirit and the mind, then our bodies. We must be conscious of what we put into our mind/body temple, which is also especially important when our soul ties are activated. Stimulating you intellectually is my desire. The more dedicated we are, the better our life will be.

I believe in healthy living which takes will power and accountability. We can support each other. The healthier we are, the longer we can pleasure one another, and the higher our vibration stays together. This is something I strive for.

The best part of sex for me starts with my mouth. The ancient Kemetians (Egyptians) say that a woman's sexual energy starts in her mouth. There is a gland that is stimulated in her mouth that gets her excited, allowing that energy to work its way from the mouth, to the breast, ending at the portal.

To my future wife, "I can say now that I adore your body because it fits me and is reserved for me in Yahawashi's name. Even if you have some insecurity, as we all do, I say this unequivocally, I will love every part of you, from the top of your crown to the bottom of your feet. *Baby, let me love you."*

I mentioned how broken-hearted I was to read that some women did not have orgasms and/or faked them. I did not get it then, and it is certainly unacceptable now. I want to edify you with my tongue. I desire to speak to you in heavenly places. *Let me be the one to give you everything you want and need.*

Speaking to my women friends, they have often ignored their own desires in favor of not hurting their mate's feelings/ego, which is counterproductive to their satisfaction. In truth, an alpha male is not concerned with his ego, especially if it diminishes his partner's sexual ability to let go, be free, and be completely and totally satisfied. *Let me be the one to give you everything you want and need.*

Exploring our sexual vibration around the world where different vibrations are harnessed, will activate different parts of our creative and intuitive mind and body, with multiple and simultaneous orgasms. Like Chris Rock says, "I want to be going and 'cumming' with you."

Corner Man

"I would go where you lead. I'll be right there in time of need. And when I lose my will, you'll be there to push me up that hill." – Aretha Franklin

Facebook Post Six: *I will be your biggest supporter and confidant. I will always actively listen to you, even when you repeat yourself or give me friendly reminders.*

Growing up, I had a fascination with fighting. I think I had a Napoleon complex, not to mention that I grew up around a lot of boxers. My uncles and extended cousins were talented and gifted amateur boxers; and man, they were beasts in the ring. Back in my day, learning to box taught us how to defend ourselves, and boxing was a way out of certain environments where other opportunities did not exist. Boxing, not guns was considered a badge of manhood, courage, and strength. Long before basketball and baseball were the sports of choice for young black men, it was boxing.

And I was a rather good boxer; I had 'good hands' as they would say. I was fast and usually struck first, especially in a street fight. It was always about protecting me and the people I loved. Today is no different. As I have grown older, I have discovered that Black women are the least protected in our society, while being the most desired, secretly. Two things that most women want are to feel safe (physical safety), and secure (comfort, protection, respect, and loyalty).

I know that many Black women feel disappointed, discouraged, and unsafe because society tries to define you as uneducated, overeducated, a teen mother, dark, light, fat or skinny, all to marginalize you. Though you may have been abused, oppressed, devalued, or assaulted, society says, "Get over it."

You as Black women have carried so much of our struggle on your backs just to survive by all means necessary. I see the necessity to deny the feminine part of you, trying to survive in this male dominant world, or because some paternal authority said it was wrong to show self-love. Maybe, it is because the last generations of males have not shown up for you such that so many women choose a male who does not require the feminine part of yourself that you subconsciously denied. It shouldn't have to be this way.

You are stronger and greater than anyone can imagine. Yet, many men do not know the difference between how you are treated, what you are up against, how it makes you feel, and what we can do to make it better.

A great boxer is not great unless his corner man is also great, because the corner man supports and helps secure the dream. It is definitely a team effort.

Muhammad Ali, the greatest boxer of all time, was one of my heroes. He chose not to reject the man he was. He rejected those who said he was wrong to speak his truth, especially about the "Negro" people. I applaud him despite many non-blacks, as well as his opponents, being terrified of him. Ali demanded this of himself: to connect to his truth and purpose. Each time Ali went into the ring, he fought with purpose and confidence. In his corner was Drew Bundini. Even with so much talent, Ali confessed to Bundini that he was scared to death every time. Ali said of Bundini that he was a great motivator and an inspiration, and I cannot help but see the balance Bundini brought to Ali. Bundini was in the corner shouting out guidance like, "Duck and weave," "Pull your punches Champ," "Get off the rope," "You are the Greatest! Now show them what you are made of."

I want to be your corner man because when you go into the ring and battle, oftentimes suppressing your pain round after round, playing defense on the ropes because the body blows are too much to handle, it is essential to our fight that I am there for you after each round. Come into the corner, sit, and let me be responsible for preventing and treating the emotional, spiritual, and sometimes physical damage from your cuts and bruises. Let me handle the swelling with a firm pressure to reduce any impairment to our vision. I am your cut man, coach, and hype man all in one. I know what you are up against, and I will never throw in the towel.

It is my duty to protect and keep you safe, and to encourage you to do your best. And, sometimes your best is whatever it is for that moment. I got you for all the moments you may fall short. The battle is ours. We are a team, and when the team works, the relationship works. I am your corner man.

A corner man anticipates, recognizes, and respects the needs of the fighters; from their temperament, to how they prepare for the fight, to an exercise regimen and diet – what they put in their temple. I am a believer in The Most High, and I too come into the fight prepared to support, just like a corner man. I will educate myself to understand your intimacy level, know your love language, and how to feed you both spiritually and emotionally. When we are prepared like a fighter, THE MOST HIGH will never put anything on us that we cannot bear. *Yahawah got us, pushing, and guiding us up the hill.*

I use Ali as the example because of the faith, integrity, and loyalty that he demonstrated to his corner man when he could have chosen not to. Bundini and Ali fell out when Bundini had an addiction for a short period when Ali could not box due to Ali's refusal to fight in Viet Nam. When it was time to get back into the ring, Ali accepted him back into the fold. I suspect this is because Ali understood that they were a team despite their falling out. Both understood that the greater good was more important than personal gripes.

In relationships, there will be some falling out from time to time, but I want you to understand, as your corner man, it is my duty to make the adjustments needed to protect our goal to win with our integrity intact. *Forgiveness does not change the past, but can present a better future.*

I see the greater good in creating a safe and secure environment because when the Black woman is cherished and empowered, so is the family and our nation. *Action is the greatest truth.*

Fully Loved

"Each moment with you is just like a dream to me that somehow came true. I know tomorrow will still be the same 'cause we've got a life of love that won't ever change." – Luther Vandross

Facebook Post, Day Seven: *"I commit to love you according to "The Four Agreements," (Don Miguel Ruiz) and to satisfy your love language. Therefore, I will make no assumptions, take nothing personally, be truthful with my words, and do my best."*

Imagine the perfect dream relationship. You are happy with that special person who you chose and who chose you. Now your life of romantic bliss begins. Nope! **You forgot about ego.** It comes along with us and our relationship morphs because of it. Typically, we start trying to make changes in the other person, so that they fit our own ego.

We must break down the fantasy of love and stop being ruled by ego. Understand, the mental trauma we have experienced in the past has limited us from being our true selves. We often have vacant-esteem that prevents many of us from loving each other because our self-esteem has been lowered by the onslaught of outside forces bent on keeping us apart. I want our love to be realistic, not based on ego and fantasy, because most relationships are not.

The Roots

As Black men in America, we have been denied our rights as men based on the continuous infiltration of the white patriarchal culture's idea of us since slavery. As a result, our identity has been "created" through a faulty prism, identifying us by our sexuality. We were made "indispensable" due to our sexuality - the ability to use our tool to buck and make babies. Coupled with high levels of stress based on racial terror, our ability to fully love is battered. *In order to fully love you, we must be healed and become whole.*

The European system has mistreated humanity and has destroyed the ability to sustainably build and maintain a solid family structure. Keeping the family apart, promoting strife, and suppressing our ability to provide for ourselves creates lack/insufficiency. All of this kept us subjugated. Though the physical chains may not be seen, the structure of oppression remains. **NO MORE!**

We must be productive and purposeful in order to create a meaningful legacy, which means we must actively make our lives balanced, honest, and transparent to fully appreciate, love, respect and accept each other.

Men, Black men, cannot continue to be defined by what society once prescribed. We must claim our positions as men, as providers, and as the chosen.

The Enmity Must End

We often are pitted against each other due to the application of the concept of misandry; the hatred of men. When our Black Queens validate this belief, in many ways, the white male dominant culture benefits, and we lose collectively. The structure that keeps us unable to build economically as a family, is not a game; it is a paradigm by design. The white propaganda narrative about our Blackness designed to have absent dads, and the false creation of the angry Black woman syndrome, can no longer be our story. Let's make it righteous.

Free the Captives

Our journey should never be about position, imitation, materialism, wealth, likes on Facebook, views on Instagram, nor the weight of the great beyond, of heaven's *"by and by"* from the pulpit.

Scripture says you are a witness in your life, not your lips. Unfortunately, some churches are commercial theater. Some have signed on to mis-educate, and negate us of our rightful place in scripture, misidentifying our roles to each other and the world. Scripture also tells us not to lean on our own understanding; in other words, do not limit yourself to what society or man or manipulative teaching has espoused. Find a Spiritual center that will teach you the truth of your position in the Tanakh. When you know who you truly are, and you understand that you are a child of The Most High, you will truly be free.

Take A Stand

I wondered as a young man, what that iconic sign, "I AM A MAN," held by Black men in the 60's meant. *We were being limited and denied our true identity and humanity as Black men.* Those powerful Black brothers were standing up to change that. The sign is also a reminder of what we need from our Queens. The love you express to us when the world does not, reminds us we are still men.

So, when the world tries to destroy our manhood and womanhood, we must be united and fight the system together. Therapy, often considered taboo in our community, works with our traumas individually and collectively; we can use it as a tool to fight for the sake of our survival.

Yahawah created love and companionship; therefore, it is non-negotiable. Spirit will not survive without us in the equation. A part of loving you Black Woman is looking out for your best interests through my healing. It's The Most High's hope (faith, love, confidence, expectation, courage) that dwells within us. Let us do our best. Let us speak the truth. Let our words mirror our actions toward each other.

True power will be ours once we realize what we are up against. Tupac sang, "Me Against the World," let's get it together, and be "Us Against the World." Let us learn to love on, and for each other. Let us be worthy examples for others to mirror.

The moment we choose to love The Most High, and learn to love others as we love ourselves, we have an open line of communication for blessings and favor. As we begin to renew our minds, getting wisdom and understanding, we begin to do and be better.

Let's ask Yahawah for a marriage with the one that is intended for us. Let's take our shot, together. Let's be the stars of our own heroic story, so when it is time for our close-up, we will be READY.

Section Four
With Maturity Comes...

Appreciation and gratitude for what is important;
family, belief in self and personal value, and legacy.

It's A Family Affair

We are a product of our family, and we often gravitate toward those that are like us. Yet, people often make decisions about their mates based on limited information, which is why "meeting the family" and knowing them, is important. It all matters because when you're marrying a person, you are marrying their family. You want to know what family you are marrying into; that is important because they influence your spouse, and ultimately, your marriage.

I'm sure you have heard stories about paying attention to the way a man treats his mother and other women in his life because that will show you how he will likely treat his mate. I believe this is true. And, do not forget to pay attention to the way he interacts with his father, and his extended family.

We Black people, both indigenous to America, and stolen from Africa, are naturally affectionate, emotional, and loving people; like many of our ancestral and distant cousins who still live in Africa today.

Yet, we have been affected by slavery and the influence and expectation of European culture; and are often discouraged from showing emotion and affection. Black men are told that it is not manly to cry, and we are trained to "suck it up" instead of showing our feelings of sorrow, rage, and at times, disappointment in love. I was fortunate to have men on both of my parent's sides who were comfortable greeting each other with hugs or kisses to express care. That was important because they would also get in your ass with hard truths and life lessons whenever we needed it. What they showed us and taught us helped us to survive, and ultimately, that saved lives.

We are very close-knit, and I might be biased, but our family is probably one of the strongest on the planet. We are compassionate and connected, which was channeled from Grandma. She instilled in all of us a spiritual responsibility, not only to ourselves, but to others.

Grandma was matter of fact and held nothing back because she knew authority could not be sugar-coated. She would say, "You must walk in your authority and speak passionately about things that matter."

I was also taught to speak edification into the ones you love. Grandma did this well. She knew how to be both gentle and stern while guiding us with simple pearls of wisdom. At times, I would call her daily, especially during my divorce.

I remember crying to her about not feeling loved one day.

She said, "There is a vast ocean of women who are ready to love you. Do not ever forget that you are a great catch worthy of being caught/chosen. Just be patient and love yourself; it will all come together."

I believed her simple words, and the love behind them. I was truly encouraged and felt better about myself better able to handle my difficult situation.

My uncles and aunts are role models that I studied and who were active in my maturation. *Brothas, while growing up, to be a real man, you must understand the compassionate part of your personality and your family duty to correct behavior in your brethen when necessary, with a loving hand.* I saw it, daily, growing up. There were no weaknesses in our tribe.

As a kid, I used to hang out with this group of guys. We were a band of brothers. I loved these dudes, and we did everything together. Guys in other neighborhoods did not like that we were popular, athletic, handsome, confident, and got the ladies, so they would start beef with us whenever we were at a party or just hanging out. I was the smallest, but most cagey of the group, and I loved to fight. It goes back to the Napoleon complex.

However, whenever we were out, I followed the rules set down by my uncles and father to always be observant, stay in the background, speak less, and listen more. I always found myself at the back of the crowd, checking for dudes who might want to beef. I am still that way, not the beefing part, but protective of and sensitive to those I cherish.

I learned later that in wolf packs, the alpha wolf is the lone wolf at the end of the pack. He controls everything. This position decides the direction and anticipates the attack because he controls from the rear. This alpha wolf concept, from Rudolph Schenkel's "alpha" wolf expression studies was developed 1947. David Mech's improved concept fits a more precise ideal of the alpha. I like to think that you can count on me based on this outdated study. I was trained for this long before Denzel Washington in *American Gangster* coined the phrase, "The loudness Nigga in the room is the weakest." In other words, I got you boo; I am your protector in deeds and not just words.

You can expect nothing less than my loyalty and devotion, my love. As your King, I am responsible for learning how to meet your needs.

Elements

Seven Aspects

I name them because I believe them to be instrumental in creating a successful partnership. They are the foundation, and once the foundation is set, it is more difficult to disrupt or destroy the building.

1. Mutual admiration and respect.
2. Active sexual fulfillment and adventures.
3. Home support – providing a sanctuary.
4. Being attractive, understanding her femininity and attractiveness; this means inside and out. Beauty is outward and inward.
   a. Inward beauty is showing compassion, being sensitive to the needs of not just yourself, but also us, those around us, and Black people as a collective. It is also expressing kindness when no one is looking; saying what she means and meaning what she says.

b. Outward means she enjoys looking good and takes care of her outer appearance from nails and hair to overall hygiene. She wants to look good for herself and her man, and she is aware that what is going on inwardly, affects what is seen on the outside.

5. To be health conscious, which includes being fit, healthy diet, and having fervent habits like prayer/ mediation and some type of exercise/exertion routine.

6. Being intelligent, to the point of seeking information; she is not just satisfied with what people tell her. I need stimulating conversation.

7. Companionship – The first time I heard the phrase 'creature comfort' I was lying in bed; the comfort of the bed, the intimate conversation and the physical touch provided a certain peace over me. This is part of what I enjoy about companionship. Each person should be aware of what they envision in terms of sharing space, thoughts, ideas, and dreams with another. Companionship is more than just sharing a house; it is inclusive, peaceful, and filled with loving intentions and solace or just the opposite. Be sure that you and your partner share enough in common that make you comfortable with each other because what you think, do and feel will determine the quality of your relationship.

Words of Counsel

Advice to Daughters/Women

The following is information I gave to my daughter at the appropriate age. I believe all young women should hear these things and take heed to them.

Do not seek a man because you are looking; a woman is to be still. Your partner is looking for you. If you start looking too, you might miss each other because you both are lost, going in different directions. Stay present once you have done the work of healing because that vibration and frequency that you give off, will allow him to find you.

Men are simple. It is not your job to fix us despite the potential we may have. You cannot make a dog meow or a cat bark. Daily, we men feel the necessity to prove ourselves by overcompensating or moving in fear instead of confidence and that gets us tripped up at times. We are not good at hiding who we are. If you pay attention, we will tell on ourselves. *Listen to what the man says and mirror that to his actions.*

Be vocal in your love making. Contrary to popular belief not all men know what they need to do to please you. It is your responsibility to instruct him on how to please you. We are not mind readers; you must communicate your needs, and when your love tank is getting low, let him know in love and gentle direction.

Prolonged conflict causes more problems. Address issues head on, and do not let it linger because we do not have long memories like you do. We have forgotten and moved on, so if you are bringing up something that was months ago, we typically do not know what the hell you are talking about; especially if we feel like everything was handled when it happened.

What About Work?

If you are passionate about being a mother and do not have the desire to have a career outside of the home, be honest with yourself and your partner up front. If money is not an issue, and you both agree to the arrangement, that is great. However, if working is part of the agreement, then it is important that you both work together for the greater good/partnership, and the financial needs of the household. Also, if your career is your passion or purpose, be sure not to sacrifice that for the sake of money; be clear about what it will take from the both of you in order to fulfill your dream.

What About Finances?

I made some mistakes not looking at the long-term financial consequences in past relationships, including my marriage. Love is not enough. We need to see past the love, so that everything we do going forward is intentional; and it must be communicated in the very beginning.

If you have bad credit, be honest about it, and be willing to improve it. Change your habits. Or, if you are divorced, owe child support, or have had a financial setback like bankruptcy or job loss, you must be willing to discuss and deal with what you bring to the table. Be willing to work on these things yourself, and if you plan to join with another, come up with a long-term plan together. Agree to financial goals and be proactive together, in order to rise above financial challenges. And don't be so eager to write a person off if they are in a temporary situation, especially if they are actively working toward bettering it. It can be easier to work together in some cases.

However, if you have not been working on these issues before you come into the relationship and are unwilling to work on them, then that tells me you are not ready to start this new business venture, called relationship.

I cannot overstate the importance of financial literacy, honesty, and transparency in every healthy relationship. To be effective, it is important to be responsible and intentional about the finances and run them like a business. I believe whoever is best suited to maintain the finances should do so, regardless of who makes the most money.

There should be multiple accounts including those which affect the future such as Stocks, IRA, Mutual Funds, Life Insurance, and Retirement/Savings. There should also be specific accounts for household expenses, discretionary spending including donations/ benevolence/slush funds, recreational/vacation funds, and individual accounts. Each person should have access to each account.

The key to financial efficiency is to not be bound by traditional perspectives of gender roles such as the man controlling the money. Reasons people do not trust each other have included infidelity, unauthorized spending that does not serve the family, and secrecy intended to control the relationship. When you are in a partnership, you must make the commitment to act in a trustworthy and responsible manner toward your partner and your family unit.

The Friend Zone

*A relationship that is open, honest, supportive,
non-judgmental, and safe is my kind of zone.*

True friendship is mutual, reciprocal, and supportive in the times of ease and emergency. That means ride or die when you have nothing, *and* when you have built something. A lot of people aren't good friends, and thus don't have good relationships because they don't know how to encourage one another through the dreams, the bad decisions, failures, and rebuilding. A real friend remains committed to the relationship when others find reasons or excuses not to. Friends are builders of confidence, encouragers of dreams, and cheerleaders over the finish line; this includes 3am on the ledge calls and 7am call backs. I believe a person who knows how to be a good friend can use those attributes to manifest into an intimate partnership, and ultimately healthy marriage.

Friends never let friends dream alone.

The bonds we have are influences in our lives; therefore, sisterhood/women bonding, and brotherhood/male bonding, can be positive for us as individuals. Like Gayle and Oprah, or the relationship of Jonathan and David; having each other's backs in Scripture. Jonathan stood up to his own father to protect his friend. I acknowledge that these friendships are important and can help women/men flourish.

We must be aware, however, that the less our respective friends know about our intimate life, dreams, and commitments to each other, the less we may need to fight off spirits wanting to see us fail with unintentional or intentional consequences. I support you in having as many girlfriends as you like, and enjoying *girls' nights* as often as you like; yet, I want to be your confidante when it is all said and done; and you're mine. When it comes down to it, I want to be your girlfriend and you, my bro; us, as best friends.

Our relationship is just that, ours. It is not a community project for everyone to chime in with their uninvited/ unwelcomed/unsolicited opinions of how we should feel and think about our relationship.

When we know each other's passwords and use the other's phone to make calls, that is an extension of our love, friendship, and true partnership. A friend calls out their friend when they are not living up to their potential. I promise that I will always be truthful, respectful, and deliberate in my words, and when I am not, I expect you to call me out, in love.

Becoming Entwined

You will be amazed at how things fall into place after letting go of past hurts and pain, attachments, false expectations and fear; as we learn to wait on Yahawah as Abraham did.

I remember when I would get my hair plaited and then twisted to make a tight fitted braid down my scalp; and the pain that came with it. Despite the pain and time it took, I looked fly, so I continued to do it. I mention this because the understanding of the Hebrew word for "WAIT" is the same for "to plait the hair", to intertwine sections of hair together so that it is tight. Can you picture it? When we plait hair, it is no longer free to be loose because it is tightened and made stronger, just like US. So, WAITING is not passive. It is serving like a waiter, but also intertwining our lives together in Spirit.

We must plait our every day with The Most High, so that we are intertwined and made stronger.

One of my favorite stories in the Bible is when Abraham's servant goes to find a wife for his master's son, Isaac. He asks to find her by way of a specific prayer; praying to his master's God that he may recognize her because he himself was not a believer. He asked that the woman say at the drinking well, "I will also give your camels a drink." Lo and behold, Rebecca spoke exactly those words, confirming destiny. He then goes to her family and explains his master's desires. They agree. Rebecca leaves with the servant. Upon meeting Isaac though a stranger, she ran into his arms, something every man wants; and he in return, takes her and loves her. It was a risk, but she somehow felt what was destined to be. Though the story does not reveal it, I have a feeling she, too, had her own specific prayer, which made her free to take a risk.

Let's Affirm This Together:

Because of the vision, The Most High has for me in His desire for love, and not just because I am lonely. I love myself, yet, I also desire the love of another, my other. That is different than being lonely or desperate. The Most High commands and expects us, men, and women to love for the sake of love, demonstrating His/Her love and vision for each of us.

A Peace of Me

I want to open up to my woman in a way that she knows,
without a shadow of a doubt, that when I say;
I like you, I see you, I got you and ultimately,
I want you, she knows it.

So, I can one day say those other important three words...
Be My Wife.

Making Marriage Last

At the heart of creating a love affair that will last forever, is seeking insight. The people we encounter offer either trauma on loop or serve as guides to a new start.

As one of my uncles often says, "The moment your pain outweighs your pleasure, you will do something different." I want you to know that you can choose differently.

We all have had people contribute to our love journey in both wonderful and dreadful ways. My unquenchable desire has always been to see Black folks win in life and love. The outcry of 'Black Love' on social media platforms is more than hashtags; for me, it is a deliberate endeavor to see our love last and flourish. Writing this book has been my sharing a piece of me; hoping it also creates peace, for us.

Giving and Receiving

Women receive our seed and give birth. If she receives confusion, hostility, and mistrust, she is given chaos, the reflection of what she received. Similarly, when given agape-unconditional love, respect, validation, and authority in a union, she births a well-tuned household, stable environment, and peace.

Men do not receive; they give. If a man wants heaven in the home, he must watch what he deposits. It is on him!

Being One, Together

Remember Black man and Black woman, keep the egos in check! Be willing to heal from trauma, work together and commit to love and to each other. When two people who love each other are on a journey together, it is not always about logic, but also letting go of the thought of perfection. It is about knowing that you are treated properly and lovingly without trying to change the other to fit into something they are not. It is about accepting each other's passion for whatever the passion is, and supporting them as long as it is not hurting you or them.

Love through your differences; as you do so, you shall rise through them as long as you remain loving, kind, generous and encouraging. Days will be challenging. Don't give up.

Yahawashi said, "Heaven is right in the midst of you." We can experience love once we awaken to our true essence permeating within The Most High's strength, love, and sound mind.

I am hopeful that you are ready. I am a believer in the words in the Tanakh of The Most High. The following scriptures are basic needs for men and women as they build a healthy union and marriage. I believe they will help keep the love tank full. *We can truly experience heaven on earth with the one that was created just for us.*

Making Marriage Last, Yahawah's Way...

Seven Basic Needs
of a Woman

Any man can make himself irresistible to his wife by learning to meet these seven basic marital needs:

1.) **Her need for leadership**. He is a man of courage, conviction, commitment, compassion, and character. He takes the initiative in cultivating a spiritual environment for the family. He becomes a capable and competent student of Yahawah's Word. He lives his life before all, founded on the Word of The Most High. He leads his wife in becoming a woman of The Most High, and he takes the lead in training the children in the things of The Most High. **(Psalm 1, Ephesians 5:23-27)**

2.) **Her need for support/admiration**. He praises her for her personal attributes, qualities and accomplishments. He admires her virtues as a woman, mother and caregiver. He openly commends her in the presence of others as a mate, friend, lover, and companion. He shows her that no one is more important in his world than her. **(Proverbs 31:28-29, Song of Solomon 4:1-7, 6:4-9, 7:1-9)**

3.) **Her need for care (romance).** He showers her with timely and generous displays of affection. He also tells her how much he cares for her with a consistent flow of words, cards, flowers, gifts, and respect. Remember: affection is the environment in which sexual union is enjoyed, and a wonderful marriage developed. **(Song of Solomon 6:10-13; Ephesians 5:28-33)**

4.) **Her need for intimate conversation.** He talks with her at the feeling level, which is heart to heart. He listens to her thoughts (i.e., her heart) about the events of her day with sensitivity, interest, and concern. Conversations with her convey a desire to understand her, not change her. **(Song of Solomon 2:8-14, 8:13-14; 1 Peter 3:7)**

5.) **Her need for openness and sincerity.** He looks into her eyes, and in love, tells her what he really thinks. **(Ephesians 4:15)** He explains his plans and actions clearly and completely because he regards himself as responsible for her. He wants her to trust him and feel secure **(Proverbs 15:22-23)**

6.) **Her need for home encouragement and consistency.** He firmly shoulders the responsibility to house, feed, and clothe the family. He provides and protects, and he does not feel sorry for himself when things get tough. Instead, he looks for concrete ways to improve home life. He desires to raise their marriage and family to a safer and more fulfilling level. Remember: The man/ father is the security hub of the family. **(1 Timothy 5:8)**

7.) **Her need for family commitment**. He puts his family first. He commits his time and energy to the spiritual, moral, and intellectual development of the children. For example, he prays with them (especially at night by the bedside), he reads to them, he engages in sports with them, and takes them on other outings. He does not play the fool's game of working long hours, trying to get ahead, while children and spouses suffer in neglect. **(Ephesians 6:4, Colossians 3:19-20)**

Five Basic Needs
of a Man

A woman makes herself irresistible to her husband by learning to meet these five basic needs:

1.) **His need for appreciation and respect.** She understands and appreciates his values and achievements more than anything else. She reminds him of his capabilities, helps him maintain his walk with Yahawah and his self-confidence. She is proud of her man, not out of duty, but as an expression of sincere admiration for the man she loves and with whom she has chosen to share her life. **(Ephesians 5:22-23,33)**

2.) **His need for sexual gratification.** She becomes an excellent partner to him. She studies her own responses to recognize and understand what brings out the best in her, then she communicates this information to her partner; together, they learn to have a sexual relationship they both find repeatedly satisfying and enjoyable. **(Proverbs 5:15-23, Song of Solomon 4:9-16, 1 Corinthians 7:1-5, Hebrews 13:4)**

3.) **His need for home support**. She creates a home that offers him an atmosphere of peace, quiet and refuge. She manages the home and care of the children. The home is a place of rest and rejuvenation. Remember, the woman/mother is the emotional hub of the family **(Proverbs 9:13, 19:13, 21:9, 19, 25:24)**

4.) **His need for her attractiveness**. She is possessed of inner and outer beauty. She cultivates a Christ-like spirit in her inner self. She herself is physically fit with diet and exercise, and she wears her hair, makeup, and clothes in a way that her husband finds attractive and tasteful. Her partner is pleased and proud of her in public, and in private. **(Song of Solomon 1:8-10, 2:2, 6:13, 7:9; 1 Peter 3:1-5)**

5.) **His need for a life mate**. She develops mutual interests with her man. She discovers those activities her husband enjoys most. If she learns to enjoy them, she joins him in them. If she does not enjoy them, she encourages him to consider others that they can enjoy together. She becomes her husband's best friend, so that he repeatedly associates her with the activities he enjoys most. **(Song of Solomon 8:1-2, 6)**

Epilogue

Seeking Her, which follows, represents the end of my Sankofa journey. The story encompasses my trek, though oddly enough, the prose was written prior to my life unfolding. The Atlantic voyage from our homeland or indigenous commencement, through trails of tears, racial terror, trauma, false narratives, it represents the spiritual navigation of every Black man's journey ends with what we do now. A Black man choosing to remember his past and prepare himself to find his love. This is tribal and this prose was written in my young adulthood before my middle son was born, and before we both adorned our loc'd crowns. The name Alimayu (God is Honored) is that of my son's middle name, who is now 26 at the age now that I wrote this piece. The system attempts to kill the Black man at his boyhood, and it is the Black man's responsibility to combat against it by being available and intentional. *My hope is that all young Black men seek the truth of their identity, healing, purpose and their one true love/twin flame. Be READY!*

Seeking Her

The summer before my senior year in college, the wind spoke in subtle whispers; its breath causing the tall blades of grass to lean to one side. The birds glide over the field in complete security. No harm comes to those who roam in this place. The center of the field stands a large oak. Its branches extend into the stratosphere. Alimayu leans gently against the tree; his lean dark muscular frame resting against its trunk. He wipes the perspiration from his forehead and regains control of his breathing. He would run almost six miles to get to this place. Removing the oversized "Rasta" cap from his head, a waterfall of dark brown godly locs tumble onto his face. Moving the hair from his eyes, he turns to face his childhood companion.

"It's been a long time old friend," he says.

Alimayu's hands slowly rub the jagged bark, "It felt as though I needed to see you before I returned to school; I am not coming back. It is time for me to receive my calling in the world."

Alimayu sits on one of the tree's protruding roots trying to understand the spirits churning within his soul. His hands begin to move across his face. He feels the rounded Solomon-like thickness of his lips, the unyielding width of his Moses nose, and the soft kinky lamb texture of his Yahawashi hair. Was the world ready for such a blunt example of The Most High?

He gazes into the turquoise colored sky, watching the ivory clouds drift toward the horizon. Things always seemed to be alive in this field. The colors were bright and filled with energy that exploded into the air, making breathing more of an adventure than a necessity. In the real world everything was distant, cold...white. Color was not a thing of joy or power. It was a curse. Alimayu felt cursed.

"How can I expect to survive in a world where I'm viewed as some sort of inferior creature? Where my very existence is associated with criminal statistics, and my power is submerged in white people's sex fantasies?" Alimayu investigates the heavens for answers. There is a timely and foretelling reply.

His mind begins to drift off, slowly toward the past. Alimayu's mother kneeling in the exact place where he sits, looking into the clouds, speaking in tongue with Spirit, and his father sat on the protruding root writing for hours and hours. The tree seems to connect the ground he sits, to the universe. The tree's limbs wrap around the sun grasping Alimayu in an eternal hug, coupling the earth with the cosmos. Alimayu's father would ponder such spiritual ideas. He made even the most cryptic images sound so beautifully real. "We are of the universe. The stars, sun, and earth float within our dark boundaries. We are children of the sun. Her energy is drawn to our Melanin; we are children of The Most High. All things live because we live."

"What does this have to do with my disturbance? How can any of this help a Black man living in a racist world?" Alimayu is baffled. His father's ideas had always confused him as a child. So, why were they coming to haunt him at this moment?

Earth.

An unfamiliar spirit began to move within Alimayu's soul. Looking down at the ground beneath him, Alimayu began to slowly pluck away the blades of the green grass. With each detaching, his spine began to straighten, and his senses became more alert. In time, he created a large patch of fertile soil. Plunging both hands into the ground, he felt warmth shoot through his veins, making him stronger. He stared at the substance in complete amazement. "We are one," he realizes, while observing the color of the earth is the same as that of his skin.

He brings the soil to his face. He smells it. The sweet scent takes his soul back to times and places he never knew.

Strong Black spirits, levitating large stones across an Egyptian desert and women, dark as coal, dancing around a fire. Flames rise and fall with each tribal chant; warriors fighting against decadent hands to maintain their life force. Freedom ships load arms, legs, and souls in shackles for sale. Strong Black spirits working as slaves on plantations; pain creating the "amazing grace" and "weeping willow," a new kind of spirit.

Alimayu pauses for a brief second noticing the change taking place within his soul. Its rhythms begin to coincide with that of the earth and the wind, creating beautifully complex musical vibrations that would make even Coltrane enviable.

He looks at his soiled hands and begins to rub the earth's remains into his loc'd crown. His soul throbs with the funky tempo of his Black spirit. He then walks into the world. He is READY.

About the Author

Randall Courtland Davis is the founder of Saints Town Productions which produces content depicting the diverse lives within Black communities for a growing audience of people who appreciate storytelling that resonates beyond cultural boundaries.

Randall attended Clark Atlanta University, is a father of three, lives in Los Angeles, California, is an avid reader of history, an outdoorsman, and sports enthusiast.

A member of 100 Black Men of Long Beach, and Black Men Build, Randall dedicates himself to bringing hope and change to all Black people of the diaspora. He also hosts Red Court TV, a thoughtful, in-depth podcast that explores the traumatic history of systematic oppression on Black love, sex, and family.

Connect with Randall through his website RandallCDavis. com, created by his brilliant child Ezra Davis.

www.ingramcontent.com/pod-product-compliance
Lightning Source LLC
Chambersburg PA
CBHW070806280326
41934CB00012B/3082